Teaching Classical Ballet

University Press of Florida

Gainesville

Tallahassee

Tampa

Boca Raton

Pensacola

Orlando

Miami

Jacksonville

John White

Teaching Classical Ballet

Copyright 1996 by John White

Printed in the United States of America

on acid-free paper

All rights reserved

01 00 99 98 97 96 C 6 5 4 3 2 1

11 10 09 08 07 06 P 9 8 7 6 5 4

Library of Congress Cataloging-in-Publication Data

White, John, 1934–

Teaching classical ballet / John White.

p. cm.

Includes bibliographical references and index.

ISBN 0-8130-1394-1 (cloth: alk. paper).

—ISBN 0-8130-1395-X (pbk.: alk. paper)

1. Ballet—Study and teaching. I. Title.

GV1788.5.W476 1996

792.8'07-dc20   95-42062

Design by Louise OFarrell

The University Press of Florida is the scholarly
publishing agency for the State University System
of Florida, comprised of Florida A & M
University, Florida Atlantic University, Florida
International University, Florida State University,
University of Central Florida, University of
Florida, University of North Florida, University
of South Florida, and University of West Florida.

University Press of Florida
15 Northwest 15th Street
Gainesville, FL 32611
http: //www.upf.com

This book is dedicated to those committed

to learning the art of teaching classical

ballet and to the students who depend upon

their teachers' knowledge and expertise.

May the spirit of Terpsichore,

the Greek Muse of dance,

touch the heart of everyone

who teaches this art.

Contents

Illustrations

Preface

As a student in southern California, I was a track athlete; friends suggested that I study ballet to improve my skills. After a year of private instruction with former Ballet Russe de Monte Carlo star Oleg Tupine, I was so impressed with the challenges of dancing that I gave up track and devoted myself to full-time study under Michel Panaieff. Two years later I was chosen to dance in a production of *Giselle* in which Alicia Alonso was appearing with her partner, Igor Youskevitch. During this experience I met my wife-to-be, Margarita de Saá, a dancer Alonso had brought to Los Angeles from Cuba.

Following the closing of *Giselle*, Youskevitch recommended that I pursue my career in New York. After a year of study with Antony Tudor and William Dollar, I returned to Los Angeles to perform in *Coppelia*, with Alonso and Youskevitch. Following this engagement Alonso invited me to join the newly formed Ballet Nacional de Cuba.

While performing in the Soviet Union during an extensive tour of Europe with the Ballet Nacional, I was particularly impressed with my visits to the Vaganova Choreographic School in Leningrad and with lessons my wife and I took with Soviet teachers.

After returning to Cuba, the artistic director of the Ballet Nacional, Fernando Alonso, arranged for a residency by Soviet Ballet Master Victor Zaplin, who worked with the company for nearly two years. Other Soviet teachers and coaches followed, who also worked with the company and helped establish the Cuban national ballet school, Cubanacan, using the Vaganova syllabus. While recovering from an injury, I was trained by Zaplin to teach company men's classes. In addition to my position of soloist, I was given the title of Maître de Ballet. I also taught a class of young boys in the new state school.

After returning to the United States, my wife and I were invited by Barbara

Weisberger to join the Pennsylvania Ballet Company, where we remained for several years teaching and working with the school and company.

In 1974, we opened our own school, the Pennsylvania Academy of Ballet, in Narberth, Pennsylvania, a Philadelphia suburb. The Academy trains over three hundred students each year, using a curriculum based on the Vaganova method. Many Academy graduates are dancing professionally in companies throughout the world and have won high honors in both national and international ballet competitions, including Varna, Bulgaria; Prix de Lausanne; and Jackson, Mississippi.

In 1986, we formed a nonprofit organization, Pennsylvania Academy of Ballet Society, to help deserving preprofessional students make the transition from talented amateur to professional dancer. Through a special training program, participants are helped to develop their talents and achieve their goals. We have placed over fifty of our dancers in professional companies.

For nearly two decades I have conducted seminars on the Vaganova teaching method for over four hundred teachers from all over the United States. From the seminars evolved the idea of creating a book that would help readers understand that excellence should be the goal of all ballet teachers. Writing the book has been more than just a labor of love. It is a deeply felt statement of the importance of learning how to teach the art of classical ballet properly.

ACKNOWLEDGMENTS

Words fail to convey the gratitude I feel toward my wife, Margarita de Saá, who gave up her country and performing career to become my companion and collaborator. She has helped make my life and work joyful and inspiring.

I would also like to express deep appreciation to Richard White for his thoughtful ideas and suggestions, and especially to Constance Goodwin for her expert editorial assistance.

Introduction

To live is to move;
without movement there is no life.

Igor Aleksandrovich Moiseyev

Excellence achieved by students in any field depends upon the competence and dedication of their teachers. Those who wish to become effective teachers must obtain the expertise required to guide the students in their care. *Teaching Classical Ballet* was written for those interested in pedagogy and to help serious teachers learn how to teach the art more effectively.

The primary audience of this book will be classical ballet instructors. However, it may also be helpful for those engaged in other teaching professions, since sound methodological principles may be transposed to other fields. And the book will be useful to everyone connected with dance education and the art of classical ballet.

The broad scope of this manual makes it impossible to resolve every question concerning sound teaching methods. Therefore, I do not attempt to cover every issue in depth. Instead, I point out major areas of concern and suggest directions that readers can follow to become more effective teachers.

My perspective derives from over thirty years of personal contact with the Vaganova method of teaching classical dance. While other methods may produce good results, I have found that the system created by the great Russian pedagogue Agrippina Vaganova has demonstrated an impressive history of success in consistently training many of the world's greatest classical dancers.

Rudimentary teaching skills may be acquired with minimal formal train-

ing. However, advanced teaching knowledge, especially that dealing with performance artistry, can be learned only through studying pedagogy with a
master-teacher.

Many segments of this book deal with advanced teaching concepts. These
will, of course, be helpful for professionals who are concerned about preparing students for careers in classical dance. However, the book also contains
valuable information for those who work at the grassroots level. Regardless of
their chosen level, all teachers will find insights that could be applied to their
individual circumstance.

The reader will find that I use the terms *classical ballet, ballet,* and *classical
dance* interchangeably. The term classical dance is widely used in all the
countries of the former Soviet Union.

The book is divided into two interrelated sections. Part 1 is a discussion of
the *art* of teaching dance and what it means to be a master-teacher. Part 2
discusses the *science,* or practical application, of teaching, including specific
guidelines for novices and professionals.

All the photographs are by Deborah Boardman and Tim R. Early and the
drawings are by Stephen Early. The models are Theresa Lynch, Elizabeth
Baker, and James Buckley.

PART ONE *The Art of Teaching*

CHAPTER 1 *The Master-Teacher*

A teacher affects eternity.

Henry Adams

In any pursuit where refined skills are necessary, there must be teachers capable of imparting the knowledge that students need to achieve their fullest potential. In the arts, great teachers help budding artists capture the full essence of their art, not merely the craft.

Teachers capable of teaching the highest levels of excellence, whom I refer to as *master-teachers*, have several important qualities in common. The process of acquiring these qualities requires that aspiring master-teachers already possess a deep desire to master the necessary teaching skills, an ability to empathize with students, and an intuitive faculty.

In dance, master-teachers are able to recognize genuine talent that may be obscured by careless teaching, thoughtless guidance, or undesirable traits of character. They have the ability to visualize the essence of the basic principles of the art and convey these mental images to their students. They are able to impart the knowledge that talented students must have to develop their full capability. And master-teachers demonstrate the ability to help their students learn to love not only the art of dance but also the learning process.

In addition to these general qualities, master-teachers are able to guide students skillfully through initial motor-coordination stages to consummate artistry. Master-teachers also have the ability to help novice teachers cultivate the art of pedagogy. And, finally, master-teachers constantly search for ways to propel their students toward the heights of artistry.

3

Most good teachers exhibit elements of the above abilities. However, teachers who understand how to guide their students toward excellence and artistry are exceptional. This special ability stems from self-discipline and dedication, a deep love for dance, and an appreciation for the grandeur of the human spirit. Those who aspire to become master-teachers must probe deeply into the core of the art. I believe that excellence in teaching can be found only at this level of dedication.

In dance, as in any specialized field, in-depth probing can be likened to plunging headlong into a complex maze, relentlessly searching for the maze's center through its intricacies and subtle secrets. Paradoxically, in spite of this seemingly complex search, good art is usually uncomplicated. During my more than thirty years of searching I have found that art's most effective statement is made through the artist's simple, uncluttered expression.

Most great artists have one thing in common. They are obsessed with an all-absorbing passion to reflect the beauty and truths inherent in their art. They also understand that refining technique frees them from the limitations that prevent their being able to express those truths.

After obtaining professional experience or earning a university dance degree, aspiring teachers should search for a master-teacher with whom to begin their journeyman teacher training. They should look for someone who demonstrates an ability to guide people through the transformation from talented beginner to accomplished advanced student, from advanced student to artistically expressive professional dancer, or from competent instructor to inspirational teacher or respected ballet master. Master-teachers have the capacity to show students how to plumb the depths of their abilities and explore new artistic realms.

In the skilled and caring hands of master-teachers, even marginally talented students and teachers may blossom into proficient professionals. Raising the commonplace to a level that surpasses all expectations is a talent unique to master-teachers. Another responsibility of the master-teacher is to motivate students and novice teachers to eliminate or reduce their weaknesses and extend the boundaries of their previously perceived limitations. The master-teacher should also have an instinctive ability to detect each student's special qualities and each novice teacher's latent capabilities.

In classical ballet, previous study with a famous teacher, attending a well-known school, or possessing a professional dance resume or an accredited degree in dance are not in themselves sufficient qualifications for teaching. Teaching, especially at the master level, requires study, hard work, and discipline. Therefore, in addition to knowing the basic material, one must learn *how* to teach. Knowledge of related skills, such as performing or choreographing, are only the foundation on which teaching skills may be developed.

The great pioneer of dance Carlo Blasis wrote in his 1820 treatise on dance theory, "A teacher without practical knowledge is incapable of transmitting to the student the true principles of fine execution which lead to artistic success."

In this manual I have separated the art of teaching dance into the following five levels and their requirements:

1. The hobbyist: basic body coordination and fundamental knowledge of music.
2. The dancer: exceptional body coordination, advanced technical grounding, and above-average musical knowledge.
3. The professional dancer: body, technical, and musical mastery plus artistic proficiency.
4. The dance artist: body, technical, and musical mastery plus artistic superiority.
5. The creative dance artist: body, technical, and musical mastery plus artistic superiority and expressive invention.

Every teacher may not be motivated or equipped to instruct at all five levels, just as not every student aspires to attain the ultimate heights of creative artistry. However, all teachers should be proficient at the level that they feel comfortable with.

In searching for a master-teacher, one must carefully scrutinize teachers who work only with talented advanced students. It is likely that many of these students have already received some (or all) of their basic training from other teachers. Giving lessons to students who have already progressed to an advanced or preprofessional level requires far less expertise than might be expected. One must learn to distinguish between lesson-givers and teachers. Also, highly gifted students are able to attain some degree of proficiency and success due to their natural gifts, despite receiving mediocre instruction. It is a sham for teachers to claim such students as products of their teaching.

On the other hand, it requires a greatly talented teacher to guide students to success who come to the art with innate personal or physical limitations. The ability to show students how to rise above their limitations is usually encountered only in a master-teacher. Great teachers do not require adulation or acknowledgment of their abilities. Their students' achievements are sufficient confirmation.

As you observe teachers at work, focus your attention on their actions and how they communicate with their students during the lesson. Try to do this over a period of time. Do not be overly influenced by such exoteric trappings as the location of their studio or the studio's expensive decor. Other unimportant details include such things as the number of students enrolled in a class; the teacher's accent, physical appearance, or personality; how well the teacher dances while demonstrating; autographed celebrity photos on the walls; or "name" dancers who may be in class. All such influences are peripheral, and only provide an entertaining atmosphere. One must develop the acumen to see beyond such facades.

It is commonplace for American students to have *many* teachers during their years of training. Rather than providing enrichment through a variety of ideas, this method more often results in confusion and lost time due to the imposition of conflicting theories on impressionable students' minds. Students should never be placed in a position where they must judge the validity of their teachers' theories or compare their methods.

It is virtually impossible to gauge the abilities of a teacher based solely upon the students in a class at any given time. Attempting to evaluate a teacher by observing one or two lessons is valid only if the students have been under that teacher's tutelage for a period of time. Otherwise, earlier training received from former teachers will likely have a residual influence on the students' development and progress.

Major dance centers attract teachers and talented students. For example, New York is the dance mecca, and dozens of teachers compete with each other to attract these dancers into their classes. Most of these students have received several years of training, arriving in New York after they have already developed a degree of competence and self-confidence. One reason for traveling to such a center might be to study with a "name" teacher, or to attend a particular school, or to be close to jobs and choreographers.

It does not require great teaching ability to give lessons to already well trained professional dancers and talented advanced students. However, it does require considerable ability, knowledge, and effort to develop a progressive curriculum that brings out the full potential of beginning and intermediate students over a period of years.

There is a vast difference between "lesson-givers" and "teachers." Classes taught by lesson-givers are usually devoid of planning, which is evidenced by a lack of attention to detail and logical progression. Sometimes their combinations are uncomfortable to perform and don't make visual or dynamic sense, while at other times their improvisations may be spirited and fun. In any case, students who desire to develop their full potential should avoid lesson-givers and search out master-teachers. Otherwise, they may be compromising their futures and their chances for achieving the high goals they have set for themselves.

Unfortunately, prosaic lesson-givers abound. Even well-established company schools and major dance centers are not exempt. Novice teachers, beginning students, and parents must exercise wisdom and discrimination in searching out knowledgeable and dedicated master-teachers. The following guidelines will help in making that crucial determination:

1. Master-teachers' classes are never overcrowded.
2. Master-teachers take time to space their students at the barre, in the center, and especially during the allegro sections of the lesson.
3. Master-teachers provide a barre that lasts no longer than forty-five minutes for elementary students and approximately thirty minutes for advanced students.
4. At least twenty minutes are set aside for the allegro section of each lesson.
5. Master-teachers maintain a discernible theme throughout each lesson, showing that they have given previous thought to the lesson and have determined a basic lesson plan.

6. Master-teachers conduct their lessons using a logical progression of exercises. Each lesson is treated as a building-block in a logical program designed to reach a predetermined goal in a predetermined length of time.

7. How are the students dressed? Are bodies covered with warmers, plastic pants, and sweat suits bunched around the ankles, knees, waist, shoulders, and arms? These are often indications of students' embarrassment about unwanted extra weight. Master-teachers insist that students correct their eating habits instead of covering up the evidence of excesses.

8. The lesson's pace will obviate the necessity to use warmers to maintain body heat.

9. Master-teachers pay careful attention to details, such as:
   a) keeping the rib cage closed;
   b) keeping the abdomen and lower back lifted;
   c) strictly maintaining the fundamentals of the basic stance (TBS);
   d) stretching the feet, straightening the knees, and keeping the thighs turned out.

10. Master-teachers stress a positive environment and constructive working atmosphere.

11. Master-teachers emphasize such qualities as artistry and nobility during their classes.

TEACHER CREDIBILITY AND PREPAREDNESS

I urge all teachers to work toward adopting the above master-teacher prerequisites. Those who aspire to that level serve their students best, because they are committed to giving their students the very best education possible. Master-teachers and master-teacher aspirants assiduously monitor the quality of their teaching to ensure that their lessons never degenerate into learning by rote. This is done by regularly reviewing their goals during each series of lessons—*preparation and planning!*

Teachers should remember that, for most beginning and intermediate students, dancing onstage in front of hundreds of spectators seems like an impossible dream. This is why master-teachers recognize the importance of setting immediate and long-range goals for their students that lead them toward ultimate technical perfection and artistry.

An immediate goal might be a relatively minor challenge, such as maintaining a perfectly level elbow in second position, or keeping the shoulders down while executing a port de bras, or raising today's best extension just one-quarter inch higher than yesterday's. Or perhaps it will be a bolder challenge, such as finding complete equipoise at the end of a diagonal of chaîné tours en pointe, or controlling a series of sixteen consecutive grandes pirouettes. The intensity, quality, and persistence of a teacher's encouragement and insistence are usually the key to a student's attainment of such goals.

In your role as teacher, nearly everything you tell your students will be taken as gospel. In your daily interaction with students, it is unwise to respond casually to sincerely asked questions. If you do not know the answer, don't improvise just to get yourself off the hook. Instead, explain to your students that you will research the question. *Then do your homework!* Nothing will erode your credibility more quickly than to have an improvised answer found faulty by a zealous student who looks to another authority to verify what you have said. Your students must be able to rely absolutely on what you are teaching them. They should understand that you will help them answer every question and solve all problems.

Use accurate terminology in your teaching. In ballet, where French terms are commonly used worldwide, it is better not to attempt to use classical terminology if you are uncertain of what you are saying or how to pronounce it. If you have any doubts about a word or phrase, check a good ballet dictionary.

Another way to lose the confidence and esteem of your students is to continue dancing with, or in front of, them when you are no longer practicing the regimen necessary to dance well. Common sense requires retired dancers to be especially thoughtful about donning tights and leotards. Drooping elbows, rigid fingers, and loosely stretched feet and knees are not the images we want to leave with our students. This advice applies to *all* retired dancers—even former soloists and principals of major companies—who retire from the stage and choose to contribute to the art by teaching or coaching. Allow the performer's spotlight to dim gracefully. Let your students see you at your best and imagine how great you once were. Concentrating on the demands of this new direction you have chosen requires you to focus on developing the skills to help the new generation of dancers. If you do this, you will continue to grow artistically. You will also find that, although you have left the stage, you have not lost the stage.

A teacher's ability to communicate with students can transmit bad habits as readily as good ones. Students often attempt to emulate everything they see, especially when a teacher commands their respect and admiration.

Think through all exercises and combinations completely before offering them to your students. Although improvisation and spontaneity have their place in art, that place is not during the dance lesson, especially at the elementary or intermediate levels. Improvisation should be used with caution even at more advanced levels. Once the planning is done, *explain* precisely what you want done. Practice the discipline of formulating clear mental pictures of your explanations. *Demonstrate* only what is necessary to illustrate your explanation. Resist the temptation to extend simple demonstrations into performances. Then *guide* your students through the exercise, demanding from them a conscientious and precise execution. Remember: explain; demonstrate; guide.

INSTILLING CONFIDENCE

Beginning students generally lack self-confidence; therefore, it is the teacher's responsibility to help them attain this invaluable attribute. Most students gain self-confidence in direct proportion to the immediate goals they attain, coupled with the knowledge that they are progressing steadily toward their ultimate goal.

Self-confidence, based on the ability to master even the most difficult challenges through daily progress, is essential for coping with the many pressures of a professional company's demanding schedule. Students must become confident that they have the ability to solve any problem they face. This confidence is an outcome of the master-teacher's positive approach to teaching. Rather than harsh criticism, the constructive actions and attitudes that teachers impart will help pupils achieve an awareness of their capabilities.

Each student deserves and needs encouragement. The master-teacher acknowledges competent performance, compliments significant improvement and strong effort, but reserves enthusiastic praise for extraordinary achievement. This graduated way of acknowledging a student's performance is designed to help her realize that rewards come from achieving seemingly unattainable goals through self-discipline and great effort.

The great Soviet ballerina Galina Ulanova said, "Whenever we dig down into the achievements of a creative artist, we invariably trace them to the beginning of all beginnings—labor."

COOPERATION AND COMPETITION

During their lessons master-teachers maintain an atmosphere in which students are mutually supportive of each other. Teachers should clearly distinguish between excellence-focused and winning-focused competitiveness. Competing *against* others engenders the attitude that one is trying to come out on top, to win something. Competing *with* others helps everyone reach higher individual levels of excellence.

Cooperative competitiveness prepares students to become members of dance companies that are imbued with a wholesome family atmosphere. Such companies, rare indeed, are usually headed by experienced and knowledgeable directors who understand the emotional needs of their dancers. These companies can provide lifelong artistic homes for dancers who maintain the spirit of collaborative competition. Unfortunately, too few of these companies exist in the dance world.

The stepping-stones toward becoming a professional dancer impose several competitive situations. The first is auditioning as a child to get into a top dance school. The next may be competing for the teacher's approval. Then students must often compete for roles in school productions. They must also compete for the respect of their peers.

Later there are more intense levels of competition, such as auditioning for national and international competitions. And for students attempting to make the transition to professional dancer, auditioning for a professional company is the ultimate competition. Here they put all their hopes and dreams on the line. For many, this competition has the intensity of a do-or-die situation.

Competitive situations continue even after signing a contract with a professional company. They include such challenges as moving up within the company from corps member to soloist to principal, being noticed by choreographers, and competing for roles that others covet.

Entering these competitive situations with a positive attitude is healthy and beneficial. However, negative competitive attitudes are most common today, particularly in large companies. Dancers often feel pressured to use all sorts of tricks to get attention. Some may be relatively harmless; others can be insidious. In either case, such tactics should not be a requisite for success in any endeavor. This situation often causes gifted young performers to flash with momentary brilliance, then to fade quickly and burn out. Sometimes inexperienced dancers find they cannot cope with the jealousy and negative attitudes directed toward them. A thick skin helps them deal with these realities of professional company life.

There are many instances of talented artists who are lost forever. Sometimes they are exploited by others, or they become victims of their own vulnerability. Attitudes based upon negative competition almost always work against young artists' attempts to attain their goals. Teachers who allow their students to develop this perversion of competitiveness are doing them a great disservice. Such teachers are establishing built-in handicaps that may cause their students serious psychological and emotional stress later on.

Master-teachers thoroughly prepare their students to meet and cope with the perverse side of competitiveness. Students must realize that in ballet, just as in all life pursuits, there are inevitable disappointments. Maintaining one's equilibrium under stress is an important lesson to learn. It is also important to remind students that many qualities associated with artistic pursuits can be refined outside of the ballet studio.

A conscientious teacher might need to administer some occasional "tough love" with students who are having an attitude crisis and are alienating other students or teachers. Though I certainly support teachers taking extra time with problem students, I urge you to spread your attention equally, keeping in mind, however, that you cannot make a silk purse from a sow's ear. I also advise you to distribute your pearls of wisdom sparingly. Your supply may not be unlimited.

You may occasionally have a student who finds it difficult to interact positively with others. Rather than putting up with the negative effect on the rest of your students, it may be better for everyone if such students are suspended from your studio. They might need to seek a different atmosphere in which to work or possibly even consider an altogether different pursuit.

FRIENDLINESS VERSUS FAMILIARITY

In the arts, it is not just technical expertise and experience that separate ordinary teachers from master-teachers. Master-teachers' perceptions are more profound, and true pedagogues work continually to elevate their understanding of the art. This includes their interpersonal relationships.

In the office and lounge, as well as in the classroom and dressing room, let students know that you respect them as individuals and not just as dancing machines. Make it clear that you also expect your students to respect each other.

During interactions between teacher and student, whether inside or outside the studio, a respectful, relaxed formality should be maintained. Master-teachers constantly present an example for their students to emulate. Most receptive students will respect their teacher's expertise, wisdom, and experience if such an example is maintained. In this regard, I find it helpful for students to address their teachers as "Mr.," "Mrs.," or "Madam." This should apply even to adult students who may be older than their teachers. My personal inclination is to refrain from calling teachers by their first names. Though not always the case, such familiarity may lead to respect that is only superficial.

Teachers should also give thought to the impact their personal life-styles might have on their students, since one cannot know when a chance encounter with a student outside of the studio may occur. Students often place their teachers on a pedestal, holding them in high esteem. It is important that students see their teachers as worthy of emulation in all respects. This is not meant to encourage an ivory tower relationship, but it should be part of the nurturing that takes place between teacher and student. Teachers who make this extra effort will see the positive effect it has on their students' willingness to elevate their own personal and professional standards.

NOTE TO PROFESSIONAL TEACHERS

It is important that teachers understand precisely what they are imparting (aside from the obvious technical matters) to their students, who more or less blindly rely upon them for their dance education and professional guidance. Ask yourself the following:

1. In addition to being technically proficient, are my students thoroughly prepared, artistically and temperamentally, to succeed as professional artists?
2. Do my students have that rare combination of artistic quality, musicality, discipline, and confidence that company directors are looking for?
3. Do my students maintain a consistently exemplary demeanor, whether they win or lose, in competitive situations?
4. Do my students deport themselves graciously in all situations?

If you have difficulty answering these questions, I urge you to redouble your efforts to pursue excellence by rigorously evaluating the qualities you are passing along to your students. The title of master-teacher is merited through hard work and a commitment to the art. Exhilarating, limit-extending challenges face every teacher who aspires to artistic excellence. It is a profound joy and enormous responsibility to help students achieve their goals as performing artists and, I hope, as contributors to society through the art of dance.

CHAPTER 2 *Inspiration and Motivation*

---

*To express the inner life of the human
spirit the artist does not see himself in
the art but the art in himself.*

Konstantin Stanislavsky

Where does artistic inspiration come from? What is its source? What is it that
inspires students and accomplished artists to press on toward ever greater
heights?

Most dancers have vivid memories of their first teacher, and how they felt
during their first lessons. This indicates that teachers leave a deep impression
in their students' developing psyche. Good teachers help their students learn
that inspiration comes from within.

It is wonderful to be shown our inherent power and how to reach beyond
what we believe are our absolute limits. Such nurturing leads students
through an exciting and rewarding dance experience. How fortunate it is to
begin our first lessons with a teacher who makes us feel welcome, who makes
a special attempt to help us overcome our fears, and who helps us find ways
to succeed at the tasks we thought impossible.

The teachers' role is vital. What do they see when they enter the studio for
the first class of the day? Or when they see a group of students for the first
time? Or after they have been working with their students for some time?
Cold, aloof teachers inevitably produce cold, aloof attitudes and dry techniques in their students, as do teachers who are abrasively critical or sarcasti-
cally demeaning. Such attitudes deaden the quality of inspiration.

To achieve maximum results, it is important to maintain a positive attitude at all times, even when enforcing discipline or giving critical analysis. However, in the business of dance instruction, we train ourselves to search out defects and deficiencies. Master-teachers train their eyes to detect the most subtle evidence of such problems. The proper motive should be to help students correct their problems and improve, but if we are not careful how we view our classes, we can drift into a state of negative perceptions, seeing only poorly done exercises or lazy, uncommitted students.

The master-teacher readily understands that the most productive learning takes place in an atmosphere that is positive and encouraging. Ask yourself, "How many times have I been teaching a class where the students seemed dull? Or unresponsive? Or slow to learn?" During such lessons the atmosphere is often heavy, and the students' attention seems to wander. However, later on, possibly even the next day, the same students seem to have a completely different attitude. The atmosphere is upbeat, and you are able to accomplish a great deal.

It is possible for students to feel down from time to time. Maybe they failed an exam at school. Maybe they had an argument with a boyfriend or parent. Maybe they think you don't like them anymore, because you scolded them the day before. Or maybe they just don't feel very well physically. However, such a situation is usually not dramatic enough to infect the entire class.

Check your own frame of mind. In many instances, a negative atmosphere is the result of a mood or a problem *you* have brought into the classroom. If your mental attitude is negative for any reason, this negativity will most likely be reflected in what you perceive during the lesson. "What you see is what you get" is a popular saying that is relevant.

When you feel the onslaught of a negative mood (for whatever reason), make sure that you deal with it *before* you enter the classroom. Take a few minutes in private to clear your mind and prepare for the lesson. Presumably, your students are enrolled in your classes because they trust you and consider you to be the best teacher available to them. Fill your consciousness with a positive anticipation of all the good qualities and achievements you expect to see and experience during the lesson. With this grounding, as you teach the lesson, identify your students' good qualities, rather than their defects and problems. You will discover that not only will they look better, they will usually respond to your positive attitude. And as a side benefit, the perception of your personal problems is very likely to take on a more positive outlook.

Assume that every one of your students is capable of learning. Some will demonstrate a greater proclivity for learning than others. For the most part, this is due to their innate talent or the extent of their desire and discipline. However, students have a knack for fulfilling their teachers' expectations, sensing what is expected of them, and they usually respond to that expectation.

Teachers often dismiss certain students as untalented or unteachable or lacking discipline. Imposing such labels on students will prevent marginally gifted ones from achieving their goals. They usually just give up, convinced by the way they are being treated that they are wasting time pursuing the art they love.

Increased understanding and a positive attitude go hand in hand. This applies to both student and teacher. For the teacher, attitudes brought into a classroom significantly affect the learning that takes place. These attitudes can influence students either positively or negatively.

Most teachers would like to have their classes filled with gifted and disciplined students; however, this is not a reality for most of us. Therefore, it is important to learn how to work with all ability levels. Uncovering and drawing out hidden talents is most rewarding. The ability to help students learn how to do their very best is one of the master-teacher's most valuable assets.

Another important lesson to impart to young students is that they can be proud of their own achievements, regardless of how those achievements compare to another's. It is a waste of time and energy to be concerned about the achievements of others. The daily lesson gives students a golden opportunity to work toward individual goals as they try to perfect a step or a series of movements. Attaining individual goals is a fundamental of the learning process of this particular art.

Your students' self-image is of prime concern. They must learn how to become achievers. You must help them aim higher, so they do not learn the inhibiting habit of being afraid to reach for seemingly impossible goals. Each small success will make the struggle for ever higher goals seem less futile and consequently more enjoyable.

There are many unique rewards for teachers and students. Dedicated teachers have an opportunity to inspire, guide, and mold young lives. Even if students decide not to go into dance as a career, the qualities they develop and the challenges they face in the classroom will stand them in good stead. They will be better individuals for the experience, and so will you.

CHAPTER 3

Recognizing Talent

Talent is work.

Maxim Gorky

What is talent? How do we recognize the mysterious phenomenon called genius? And how do we differentiate one from the other?

Those who attempt to define talent and genius generally agree that they are natural endowments—often describing creative or artistic aptitudes. Can they be taught? We shall try to answer this question later. But, first, let's define the two terms.

Webster's New Collegiate Dictionary says that genius is "extraordinary intellectual power especially as manifested in creative activity; transcendental superiority." Webster says that talent is "a special, often creative or artistic aptitude; the natural endowments of a person."

I have found that one of the main ingredients that separates talent from genius is that genius breaks traditional molds and creates new ones, while talent tends to embellish these new molds. The experience of participating in and seeing hundreds of performances, and working with thousands of students and professional dancers, has convinced me that genius is a unique and rare gift that deals with creative ingenuity, whereas talent relates to superior natural aptitudes. It is probably correct to say that anyone who possesses true creative ingenuity is also talented; however, one who demonstrates superior natural aptitudes is not necessarily a genius. And both talent and genius must be contrasted with ability, which relates primarily to refined skills.

It should be obvious that talented people can accomplish much more than untalented ones, if they plumb their gifts fully. With genius there is a profundity that defies intellectual analysis or explanation, whereas talent arises from a source that, though often quite extraordinary, is more easily understood. Therefore, I have not dismissed the possibility that talent's resources, though seemingly hidden, can be identified and developed. The master-teacher's challenge lies in discovering ways to accomplish this.

Using the above definitions, then, it is safe to say that neither genius nor talent can be taught in the way that technique is learned or in the way that ability is refined. Barring a complete lack of aptitude, most techniques and abilities in the arts can be taught by good teachers and learned by good students. It must be clearly understood, however, that talent in one aspect does not necessarily imply talent in another.

In the arts, *genius* is the term reserved for a person who naturally displays extraordinary talent. Statistically, a very small percentage of those who seriously study dance develop the necessary talent to become professional dancers. And of those who are sufficiently talented to become professionals, very few possess the necessary artistic sensitivity, or qualities that comprise artistry. Among those who are both talented and artistically gifted, only a small handful attain the heights that an individual is capable of reaching—true genius.

TALENT AND ACHIEVEMENT

While talent and achievement do not necessarily go hand in hand, they are related. Essential for ensuring success in dance is a *need* to dance. Desire is not enough. Aspiring dancers must also have the right physique for dance, and they must possess at least one latent talent that can be educed into a state of professional usability through a comprehensive and correct training regimen. They need extraordinary mental discipline and the ability to focus intently on the task at hand. They must also demonstrate the motivation to place the pursuit of their career above what most people consider to be a normal life.

Nearly all dance students are lacking in one or more of the above areas. If the shortfall becomes too great, the chances of professional achievement are unlikely.

There are additional essentials for dance mastery. These include several of the requisite talents refined into a state of professional usability. Also important for dance at the professional level is an intelligent and thorough approach to such aspects as the study of roles and to such mundane chores as rehearsing and making good use of the daily lesson.

Dedicated artists take extra time to discover the many subtle nuances associated with the roles they create onstage. They ask questions of the choreographer, spend time in the library, read books, watch videos, and attend live concerts of music, opera, and other dance forms. In other words, they expand their artistic horizons, rather than work with tunnel vision. Dedicated artists recognize that each rehearsal is a theatrical situation. They make full use of the opportunity to test their technical and artistic understanding of the parts they are preparing to perform. Rudolf Nureyev said, "When you study some character in your performance, you are obliged to find a basis for each movement, and without this it could have no truth. You must believe through your whole movement—otherwise it is immediately seen by the audience and everybody that it's wrong."

Rehearsals should not be just run-throughs or "marking" sessions for memory. Instead they should retain the theatrical ingredients that performance demands. Such an approach to daily work steadily improves stagecraft and performing skills. Later, when performing a role onstage, the artist only needs to concentrate on general artistic qualities. Technical concerns and the minutiae of artistic interpretation will have already been worked out in the rehearsal studio. Refined technique and artistic awareness can turn the *hope* of a good performance into a demonstration of artists' confidence in their abilities. A performing art must demonstrate the dignity and beauty of artistic expression. The audience rightfully expects to be uplifted from the mundane to a level of spiritual enlightenment. Dancing onstage is not just a question of going through steps, however brilliantly. The creative artist presents a person onstage who lives a role through expressive movement and meaningful gesture.

To place one's career ahead of what is considered to be a normal life one must have a strong desire to go beyond what is asked or expected. Such a committed artist recognizes the importance of continually resubmitting to further training at the hand of a master-teacher.

To move from technical mastery to artistry, one must refine all dance-related talents into a state of professional polish. At this level one must feel compelled to dance. True artists possess the discipline to push *far* beyond what is generally expected, so that they gain insights into the mysteries of creative experience and find ways to share these discoveries with their audiences. Finally, they continue to work regularly with master-teachers to refine the artistic nuances of roles to be performed and to keep technique at peak form.

Notice that each of the above categories leads to a different level of achievement, and there is a demand on the dancer to include increasingly higher levels of discipline. In this regard discipline should never be thought of as punishment or criticism, nor is it an attempt to suppress individual expression. The most fruitful discipline is generated from within. It is the recognition that no great achievement is possible without focused hard work.

Martha Graham said during an interview commissioned by Pittsburgh television station WQED, "Your goal is freedom . . . but freedom may only be achieved through discipline. In the studio you learn to conform . . . so that you may finally be free."

Master-teachers provide an atmosphere that promotes self-discipline. Master-teachers know that only through ardent self-discipline does mastery lead to artistry, and artistry lead to creativity. They show their students numerous ways to press beyond normal limitations and natural abilities. The experience of breaking through personal limitations and savoring excellence early in their careers instills in students the certainty that they possess the ability to attain excellence without any outside stimulus.

Definitive performances from the greatest creative artists usually come after years of repeating the same role over and over—studying every nuance, living the part, being at one with both the character portrayed and the music. This inspired identification with the artist's role-character, under the musical umbrella, results from the profound level of commitment that comes from pursuing the highest levels of technical proficiency and thoughtful artistic conviction.

Among the greatest frustrations and disappointments that confront teachers are those imposed by innately talented students who choose not to apply or develop their talents. These students waste their talents by ignoring them altogether or by not valuing them. This is tragic for them, but it is their choice and harms no one else.

However, there are also students who pervert their study into ego-inflating, "me first" activity. They are intent on seeking fame and personal adulation. This self-centered approach often causes negative ramifications that can be destructive to those who stand in the way. Such an attitude should not be tolerated. The wise teacher's policy of maintaining direct liaison with young students' parents goes a long way to protect those talents from being wasted or distorted.

Some claim that teachers bear the sole responsibility to uncover and develop talent. That assertion places a serious burden on the teaching profession. While it is true that teachers have the responsibility to offer their students the tools and guidelines to bring out and develop latent talents, the ultimate responsibility for their development lies with the students themselves.

In addition to imparting a curriculum that can develop all the necessary technical skills, teachers sometimes need to give extra time to their obviously talented students. This extra time might be spent in alerting them to the important relationship between everyday classwork and the stage, and in helping them understand the difference between quality of movement and mere technical proficiency. Only the naturally talented seem to comprehend the extreme importance of the quality-versus-proficiency dichotomy. Strangely, this comprehension is rarely intellectual. It has more to do with deep inborn feeling. Talented students show evidence of their gifts by an easy naturalness of balance and an effortless way of moving that always seems to make sense and fit logically together, without appearing affected or contrived.

During a talk with aspiring actors, the actor Martin Sheen once said, "Talent, talent, yes! *Very* important! . . . but technique sets your talent free." The atmosphere that best nurtures talent is created by the teacher who actively encourages individual expressiveness in the classroom but never does so at the expense of correct execution and the necessary focus on technical command. Such expressive feeling should be a vital ingredient of the teacher's methodology.

In class, master-teachers help their students understand that nobility and finesse are essential elements of every exercise, even the most basic battement tendu combination. Teachers who emphasize these elements in their day-to-day teaching open wide the gates that attempt to prevent the fusion of the craft of dance with the art of dance.

Once students learn to differentiate emotion from artistic expression and understand that their teachers eschew the former and expect the latter, an interesting metamorphosis often occurs. Talented students come to revel in their newfound expressiveness, while more prosaic-minded students either begin making patently awkward attempts at expressiveness or rigidly avoid letting go for fear of appearing silly in front of their peers.

The vast majority of dance students find it difficult to infuse genuine feeling into their movements. They lack grace and resist attempts by their teachers to coax expressive artistry from them. When called upon to do so, they either freeze up and become clumsy or react with an exaggerated and artificial-looking stage manner. Many of these dancers doggedly struggle through years of study, wondering why no one pays much attention to their dancing, even though they have acquired a degree of technical proficiency.

Experience has shown me that most students stubbornly resist attempts to impress upon them the importance of infusing artistic ingredients into their dancing. They mistakenly believe that if they mimic the choreographer or ballet master, artistry will just happen onstage when the curtain opens. Fortunately, the selection process imposed by most professional dance company directors eliminates most of the dancers who labor under this erroneous attitude.

From the perspective of dance at the professional level, it is usually fruitless to spend much time attempting to give artistic guidance to plodder-students. They usually prefer to work slavishly to increase the number of pirouettes or jump ever higher, or they can be found holding endless balances. Nevertheless, plodders comprise the majority of dance students. As long as they study dance for the right motives and are realistic in their aspirations, they deserve the best instruction we can provide. They are the financial foundation of most of our dance studios and comprise a large segment of our theater audiences.

Like cream on milk, exceptional talent rises to the top. It is incumbent upon teachers to provide the very best instruction and permeate their classes with a special blend of gentle but firm pressure on the students to rise to ever greater challenges—to stretch themselves to their limits—so they reach their maximum potential as rapidly and safely as possible. Helping students achieve their potential might mean moving them into a more advanced class or perhaps spending extra time with them outside of their regular class schedule.

Innately talented students rise steadily toward their full potential in an environment that encourages them to press on toward technical command and artistic expression. Only in this way do talented dancers find freedom of expression. They must learn that excellence is the only acceptable goal and that pursuing excellence should become a habit. Weak technique, even when combined with great artistic gifts, renders dancers subservient to their body's limitations and their mind's fearful reluctances.

A sage once said:

A man with great talent, who expends extraordinary effort and ingenuity in pursuit of his goals, can become a king.

A man with little talent, who also expends extraordinary effort and ingenuity in pursuit of his goals, can become a prince.

But a man with great talent who expends neither effort nor ingenuity is destined to become a pauper.

The world is replete with paupers. Let us strive to instill in our students the desire to attain one of the royal levels of achievement.

CREATIVE GENIUS AND TEACHING

Occasionally a student or a seasoned dancer is privileged to work in direct association with a creative genius. However, there is a caveat that comes with this privilege. One of the peculiarities of genius is that genius in one area of dance does not always carry over into other areas.

For example, a great dancer, a brilliant choreographer, or a superlative director may not necessarily be a good teacher. In fact, the reverse is usually the case. The restless temperament and emotions involved in the creative process often overshadow the methodicalness that is required for good teaching. The scientifically systematic type of thinker is often far better suited. Therefore, while studying with a great choreographer or a famous dancer may be compellingly exciting, their classes often lack a solid academic base.

Antony Tudor once confided in me that he really did not enjoy teaching very much. He said he taught because he could not earn a living working exclusively as a choreographer. He confessed that he rarely came to a lesson prepared in any way, but just "winged it." He gave no time to lesson planning but merely improvised. This attitude is common with many highly creative individuals when they teach.

Lessons taught by choreographers may be witty choreographic experiments, just as lessons taught by famous dancers may be fun and dancey. But such lessons often lack the methodical progressions and logical connections that students need. I have found this to be a common problem.

Students who study with a choreographer should attempt to discern whether or not their teacher is using generally accepted principles of good instruction. However, most students (even professional dancers) lack the background to make well-founded judgments in such situations. They often become so infatuated with the electric atmosphere that surrounds such famous individuals that they suspend commonsense judgment in the presence of the person's "greatness."

When pedagogic system is lacking, creative artists may experiment with new ideas or theories in direct conflict with established principles of instruction. These may later prove to be detrimental to their students. Unfortunately, because of their fame, their opinions are often accepted as the truth. Their personal eccentricities are often emulated as well. Students and professionals need guidance in this regard.

CHAPTER 4   *The Performer's Mission*

Today the most melodious songs have failed
to woo The Graces to our stage.
Thus, if the dance appeals to neither wit
nor eye, what's to ensue
Save pleasure's flight
and ennui lingering at its heels.

Fuselier

As with all performing arts, dance does not exist primarily to satisfy the artistic urges of its participants but to give pleasure and elevate the spirit of its audiences. It is commonly agreed that the responsibility of professional performers is to entertain their audiences. This may not be a universal viewpoint, but for the moment, let's consider it a given.

The creative dance artist and the choreographer assume two overriding responsibilities. One is to educate—skillfully leading the audience on a purposeful journey. The other is to inspire—guiding the audience to a heightened level of awareness. These responsibilities demonstrate the distinctions between commercial stagecraft and artistic creativity. These differences, along with the fundamental differences between skillful dancers and truly creative artists, are often unrecognized by audiences and critics.

Many dancers, as they approach the pinnacle of their profession, feel the restless impulse to modify their work to prevent boredom with the daily routine or to alter the interpretation of a role. However, creative dance artists are dedicated to refining and perfecting their work. Working within their assigned roles, they explore new artistic heights, sharing insights with their audiences.

For some dancers the motivation to perform is self-centered, while creative artists' motivations are focused on how to bring more meaning and artistic expression to their roles. Because of the wide disparity among theatergoers in their understanding of the art, each type of performer finds a supportive audience.

Some theatergoers crave the sensory thrills of novelty and flashy, physical exhibition. More knowledgeable theatergoers search for those rare artists who enliven their performances with choreographic creativity infusing artistic principles into the roles they dance. In classical dance, these theatergoers are known as "balletomanes." As such, they seek to be elevated from everyday preoccupations. They long to be inspired and uplifted by their experiences in the theater.

At any theatrical event the audience should receive a charge of enthusiasm. It might be subtle or electrifying. Creative artists remember that they not only entertain their audiences but also educate and inspire them. They accept this responsibility, not just because the audience has paid to see them perform, but because performing artists are, in fact, professional entertainers. Like other theater arts, dance is show business, and it should be the nature of those in this artistic business to make every attempt to uplift the spirit of everyone attending their performances.

It is fulfilling when there is a marriage between satisfied and stimulated audience and satisfied and stimulated artist. Performing artists should aspire to this ideal. Unfortunately, after some dancers have performed the same role many times, or must dance roles they do not particularly enjoy, their bored or unhappy attitude becomes apparent to the audience. This is inexcusable. Such dancers either have lost sight of the reason for being professional performers or have never understood it.

If artists only performed for their own enjoyment and inspiration, they would not need an audience. But since the audience is integral to the performance, it is incumbent upon the performer to come to it with a selfless and inspired frame of mind.

True artists aspire to an ideal, an ethereal transcendence that is portrayed by their work. Sometimes the display is passionate, sometimes tranquil. In either case, good art transforms the ordinary into something timeless.

THE ART OF GIVING

"Without sounding pompous, the phrase is, 'to give a performance.' It's something you give—because it makes you feel good giving it." These words spoken during an interview by the actress Anne Meara set the tone for an important attribute of every true artist.

Master-teachers inject their students with the ingredient of *giving*. This is, however, a quality seldom given importance by teachers. Occasionally teachers and coaches stumble across its benefits and are able to achieve outstanding results with their students. Throughout history this talent has been imparted by philosophers and religious leaders but seems not always to have been well understood by their followers and adherents. Giving is an essential ability for a master-teacher to develop. It is also an essential ability for a dancer to develop to reach the level of creative dance artist.

Because giving is a feeling one is imbued with, its exact meaning is difficult to convey. However, I will attempt to offer some clues, then urge you to pursue the concept on your own. When dancers give themselves selflessly to the art, they receive personal and intangible rewards in addition to the obvious accolades. Giving artists do not seek money, acclaim, or fame, although these rewards frequently have a way of finding them.

Giving has nothing to do with quantity—the amount of effort exerted during performances or the number of performances given per month. It refers to the quality of dedication that dancers give to their art, day in and day out, even when there is no audience watching, as during a class or rehearsal. Remember that creative artists in any art maintain a continuously elevated attitude, not just when there is a concert to perform. They understand that they possess an infinite supply of artistic ammunition and that giving does not deplete their artistic storehouse.

It is uncanny when you first feel the effects of giving. Those who practice it are often referred to as selfless. When such artists dance selflessly during a performance, they radiate something intangible that the audience feels. Even if this occurs during the performance of a minor role, it sometimes becomes an artist's stellar or most radiant performance. From this rare ability originates the term *star* that is sometimes applied to such artists.

There are many benefits realized by practicing a giving attitude. An often overlooked benefit occurs when giving dominates one's thought just prior to the start of a performance. One does not feel the paralyzing anxiety experienced by many performers. In place of the idea that the audience out there is judging their performance, giving-imbued artists genuinely feel that they are sharing their performance with the audience. It also eliminates the nongiving performer's often-heard rationale, "I need my adrenaline-producing nervousness to charge my batteries."

Another little appreciated benefit is that giving removes the destructively competitive drive to be the center of attention. Giving artists see clearly that their only true competitors are themselves. They are determined to challenge their own personal limits and do not have the time or interest to challenge or feel threatened by others.

Giving artists also explore realms of artistry that no one has previously explored in exactly the same way. This leads to creativity. Such dancers find something new while repeating their performance of the same role. They are not bound by rigid rules of technique or historic precedent, taking care that change must never be imposed at the expense of good taste or just to provide a diversion.

As the body weakens with the passage of time or injury, intelligent artists recognize that those doors that seem to be closing to them are, in fact, directing them toward other avenues of artistic expression—ones they may not have previously explored or considered. Being receptive to such subtle directives enables them to provide valuable service to their art in new and different ways.

CHAPTER 5

The Pursuit of Excellence

Ah, but a man's reach should exceed his grasp,
Or what's a heaven for?

Robert Browning

The terms *excellence* and *perfection* are often used to indicate unreachable goals or states of being. My search for their meanings, especially as they relate to the artistic process, has helped me discover that pursuing excellence and perfection describes a dynamic activity comprised of ceaselessly working at increasing one's accuracy, extending one's supposed limits, and eliminating flaws.

This increased awareness leads me to urge all teachers to help their students recognize that reaching toward excellence should be an ongoing life-long effort. Students should be taught that perfecting their abilities is an essential goal. Master-teachers make abundantly clear to students that they must pursue excellence *for themselves*—for a personal sense of integrity. This is accomplished by adopting the pursuit as a habit of thought, rather than the counterfeit of merely looking good "for my teacher," "for the other students to see," or "for the audience to applaud."

Students should never be allowed to settle for mediocrity. Accepting mediocrity can become an unyielding habit, and dedicated students need to be pushed toward ever higher levels of achievement. Until a seemingly insurmountable obstacle is hurdled, such pressures might be painfully against their will and cause some anxiety, but small successes help to achieve desired lofty goals. 31

Under the guidance of a perceptive master-teacher all students have the capacity to accomplish more, both technically and artistically, than if left to their own devices. Knowledgeable educators teach their students that excellence is one of the goals of focused hard work. The experience of achieving excellence through hard work helps students learn to respect and enjoy the process.

Students who learn early that concentrated, persistent effort brings noticeable improvement and concomitant rewards will develop an optimistic conviction that all goals are attainable. They will also discover that they must sometimes launch into unknown, even frightening, territory. Students deserve their teacher's respect and praise each time it is clear they are expending extraordinary efforts in their personal pursuit of excellence, regardless of how their performance might compare with someone else's.

Attaining high goals cannot happen without risk. During an interview on WNET (Philadelphia Public Television), while discussing himself as an emerging artist, actor Harvey Keitel said, "Progress demands risk."

Teachers should also demonstrate how hard students must work to make headway in their pursuit of high goals. I have seen it proven time and again that, when dedicated master-teachers serve as inspirational role models, students raise their sights above comfortable levels of proficiency and dare to strive toward artistic excellence. Master-teachers do this by giving their students inspired levels of instruction in every lesson, and letting the students know that they expect *everyone* to strive for improvement and progress toward individual goals.

THE BENEFITS OF PAIN

There is pleasure in suffering well.

José Martí

Not all types of pain are physically or emotionally harmful. Pain is an idea that is formulated in the brain. We are most familiar with physical pain, resulting from nerve stimuli transmitted to the brain from an affected body part. These stimuli are usually interpreted by the brain as negative messages that signal discord or danger. However, these nerve impulses can also be interpreted as positive messages, such as progress or success.

For the purposes of this discussion I have divided this topic into the following three categories:

1. Pain associated with physical injury—clearly a negative stimulus;
2. Pain associated with emotional anguish or distress—also a negative stimulus; and
3. Pain associated with limit-pushing effort—a positive stimulus.

It is important to learn how to distinguish between each of the above, and except where severe physical pain might cause an involuntary response, choose the appropriate response.

It is my experience that few parents teach their children, and teachers their students, how to accurately interpret these messages. The result is that most people choose to avoid whatever pain they can by eliminating as many painful experiences as possible early in life. Unfortunately, those who choose to avoid such experiences are ignorant of the positive potential that these occurrences may offer. This ignorance prompts some sad consequences.

The indiscriminate administering of baby aspirin begins this cycle. The pattern continues with more advanced remedies for pain, such as analgesics, alcohol, barbiturates, and the most damaging hallucinogens and narcotics, all taken to remove our suffering.

It is interesting to note that many parents and teachers, while failing to instruct youngsters in the potentially positive uses of pain, endorse the concept of pressuring their children for advancement in school via better grades and higher scores on exams. For example, many children are taught by parents not to be satisfied unless they receive straight A's on tests and reports. Students who excel academically accept such pressure. They invariably discover that exerting greater effort results in higher levels of achievement. The willingness to expend extraordinary effort to achieve higher goals is, without question, a desirable quality.

It is agreed that high academic achievement usually leads to acceptance by better colleges and that graduation from better colleges usually leads to better jobs and quicker advancement on the job. Our culture seems to have accepted the idea that this type of intellectual pain is an acceptable price to pay for what society calls *success*. The investment of years of such voluntary discomfort promises to return dividends of financial security, social status, and personal self-satisfaction, which all supposedly lead to future happiness.

In addition to intellectual pain, there are other socially acceptable types of voluntary pain. Competitive athletics, dieting, wearing body-shaping garments, undergoing psychiatric therapy, cosmetic surgery, religious confession, long-distance running, and biking are examples of voluntarily imposed pain. Some are physical, some mental.

Related to the aforementioned types of voluntary pain is a peculiar pain that is essential for achieving success in the arts. Dance is particularly associated with this type of pain, especially among dance artists who will not accept anything less than perfection in their art. Those unique artists who have established this high goal for themselves feel a deep personal drive to become the very best that they can possibly be, even the best there is. Such highly motivated, disciplined individuals willingly put their bodies and minds through daily discomforts, risking everything for technical command and higher artistic achievement. For them, intensely focused energy is a natural consequence of the effort they put into their activities. They get an emotional high from this extraordinary effort. This behavioral pattern becomes a habit that is formulated early in childhood and is supported by understanding parents and teachers during a child's formative years.

Among the myriad of would-be artists, seekers of perfection are a very small minority, largely due to the failure of most students' parents and teachers to show them how to use pain as an ally. Virtually every would-be artist needs early instruction to learn how to rise above mediocrity.

When discussing pain in this context, we are, of course, not referring to physical pains that stem from injuries to the body. Pains that arise from muscle strains, ruptures, sprains, and fractures are danger signals that should be dealt with therapeutically and should never be ignored or covered over with painkilling drugs. Instead, we are specifically referring to that unique kind of pain that is encountered only by a person who methodically presses hard against what the body says are its absolute limits.

Limit-pushing is unknown territory for those experiencing it for the first time. Parents, teachers, and experienced artists can tell you what they felt when they pushed into their unknown territory, but cannot tell you with certainty what you will find when you push into the realm of your absolute limits. Limit-extending is a uniquely individual experience that is interpreted differently by each explorer.

In dance, for example, limit-pushing should occur in the daily lesson where the master-teacher presses each student toward ever higher goals—not to hold back when attempting an extremely demanding dance combination, a complex leap, a continuous series of spinning turns, or a long-sustained balance. The student must be taught to attack vigorously the task at hand. This daring, courageous effort is what excites the interest of audiences and critics. The degree of daring is what separates the creative artist from the competent soloist and the soloist from the corps dancer.

The positive potential of pain is experienced by those who resolutely strive to achieve the pinnacle of any endeavor. The master-teacher's challenge is to help students find the delicate line between risk effort and potentially injurious effort.

No one should live in pain as an end in itself. This is a mistaken masochistic badge of misplaced courage. The dance artist must learn to tread this fine line accurately. The master-teacher, possessing an uncommon blend of insight, perspicacity, knowledge, and sensitivity, knows that beginning students may become somewhat frightened by their interpretation of pain impulses. Inexperienced students sense that their bodies are clearly calling out *Hurt!* and their brains are responding *Stop!*

Insist that shin-splints, strains, sprains, and tendonitis be treated immediately as warning signals from the body, which is saying, "I've been abused," "I've been manipulated badly," or "My nutritional needs are not being met."

Although I do not wish to offend my colleagues, I must state that it is reprehensible for those in positions of authority to insist that dancers under their control continue dancing while injured. An unfortunate psychological trick played upon young and vulnerable dancers by some uncaring directors is to make them believe that they will lose a hard-earned role or position if they take time off to recover from injury.

Most dance-related accidents, injuries, and disabilities are avoidable. Dancing while injured should be recognized as foolish and ill-advised, an act of ignorance, not bravery. Pride, fear, and stubborn willfulness often override wisdom and good sense when it comes to treating injuries, and they usually cause simple injuries to become chronic disabilities.

Primary responsibility for instructing young students on how to deal with injuries rests upon dance teachers or athletic coaches, who must educate their students to view their bodies as strong but delicate instruments. Like a Stradivarius violin or a Steinway grand piano, they are capable of being used hard and long but require strict levels of care if they are to perform at peak and remain sound.

Master-teachers develop tactics designed to keep their students safe, while urging them to their personal limits. Trusting students must be guided carefully into the territory of their absolute limits. In this way, injurious physical danger is avoided and the teachers help their students explore a threshold that each day is pushed back, widening the parameters farther.

While limiting parameters are pushed back, reflex pains that result from the onset of actual physical injury must be handled wisely. Such pains must always be treated as legitimate, imminent danger signals, demanding either instantaneous reduction of the activity or therapeutic attention.

Students must be taught to distinguish the difference between the brain's squawking reluctance to push ahead when it detects risk or stress messages coming from the body and legitimate physical pain stemming from actual or impending physical damage. Master-teachers understand the difference, usually because they have had personal experiences with pain, and they have the perspicacity to teach students to recognize the telltale signs that distinguish one from the other.

Careful attention and considerable effort are necessary to guide students safely through this vital aspect of their artistic training, so they can deal intelligently with the negative varieties of pain as well as take advantage of the positive effects of goal-achieving pain.

PERFECTING DETAILS

Art can only be achieved by the highest commitment to perfecting details and discarding whatever is superfluous. Art begins with grand concepts and unreachable goals. But such concepts and goals are just mental images until the coloration of details that define and enrich the idea is added.

It is said that the famous sculptor Michelangelo was completing a statue when an acquaintance came to visit. Seeing the master hard at work, the friend decided to come back later. Several days went by before he had an opportunity to do so. Noticing that there had been very little progress since his previous visit, the friend asked why he had been idle. Michelangelo replied that he had by no means been idle. He told his friend that he had retouched this part and polished another. He said that he had given more expression to a lip and more energy to a limb. Being quite unimpressed, the friend responded that these were but trifles. "It may be so," answered the sculptor, "but recollect that trifles make perfection, and that perfection is no trifle."

If one considers the magnitude of Michelangelo's genius and the high degree of perfection in his art, his statement that "trifles make perfection, and that perfection is no trifle" becomes highly significant. In essence, the master was saying that paying attention to trifling details is what transforms a grand idea or a beautiful concept into art.

Art is the result of a conscious use of creative skill. In a sense, all artists are sculptors, working to mold and chisel thought. We should ask ourselves, What is our model? Is it imperfection or perfection? Is it discord or harmony? Each of us is free to decide which model to use.

The world is continually holding imperfection before our eyes. It claims that excellence and perfection are impossible goals, and that the ultimates of harmony and beauty are unattainable—the effort too great. If we opt to take an easier path, then our lifework will be limited.

To remedy this problem we must turn our attention to the direction that leads toward our goal. We must follow the impulse of that leading. We must keep the perfect model foremost in thought and look at it continually. Otherwise we will never be able to achieve excellence or come close to demonstrating perfection.

A dancer should not expect to be significantly better during an important performance than when rehearsing or taking a lesson. Most students have difficulty understanding this idea as they grind through their daily ritual of sometimes tedious study. While students have no difficulty understanding that they must work hard to learn the techniques and other performing skills necessary to becoming professionals, it is far more difficult for conscientious teachers to instill in their students the following desire (or, better, *need*): *Never be satisfied with mediocrity!*

To become a great dancer you have to hate dancing badly more than you love dancing well. Dancing well does not begin when you know all the right steps but when the tedious and ordinary are transfigured into art.

Art is about perfection, and nothing short of that goal is acceptable. Therefore, the pursuit of excellence is essential. It can be an arduous climb. The famous actress and coach Stella Adler once told a class of budding actors, "Know what you can do, and do it like Hercules." Of course, not all students, including talented novices and working professionals, are willing to work that hard. Most see perfection as an unattainable goal and feel incapable of achieving it.

It has been argued that no one can ever achieve perfection. However, a true artist never gives up aspiring to that level of excellence. After all, if we don't strive for perfection with every ounce of energy and dedication in our being, we will never come close. Falling short of a desirable goal after expending great effort is no disgrace. Dedicated strivers will find themselves much nearer to that goal than they were before. Therefore, the struggle is important.

The struggle must be efficiently organized. Progress is essential, even though tediously slow at times. Sometimes it means taking one step backward in order to take two steps forward. Such retrograde steps might be likened to the mythical phoenix, which, after being consumed by fire, rises from its own ashes to become even more beautiful than before. At other times, as the striver arrives at the brink of a new plateau, technical or artistic progress seems almost imperceptible. However, in such instances, the striver may experience progress in unexpected areas, such as personal maturity, character development, and insight. Each new level attained along the way should be considered a period of consolidation by disciplined workers, who recognize that they are building a solid foundation upon which to base further technical and artistic advancement.

One must never allow oneself to drift into self-pity, self-condemnation, or depression. These are destructive and undermine one's progress. The climb up the mountain follows a narrow path surrounded on all sides by menacing and tempting distractions.

The greatest progress and growth are attained by those who rest upon proven principles for direction and guidance, not just upon themselves. Teachers of undemonstrated claims, no matter how popular they may be or how enticing their ideas, generally communicate their theories with adverse results due to their misconceptions and misinterpretations of correct fundamentals. Innovative opinions are no substitute for demonstrated results.

Master-teachers never attempt to control their students' minds. They entrust them to the principles they know will attain the desired goal. Teachers who divest themselves of pride and ego do the most for their students. They focus on emptying students' minds of erroneous concepts so their minds can be filled with the ideas that lead to the best results.

While the refinement of trifles helps to create art, there are also trifling distractions that hinder progress, such as petty annoyances, impatience, indifference, apathy, selfishness, and carelessness. But such undesirable traits should be of little concern to true artists-in-the-making.

There are, however, some essential personal trifles that should be cultivated. Among these are alertness, patience, discipline, and carefulness, in addition to such indispensable artistic trifles as feeling, expression, purity of line, musical sensitivity, projection, and a beautifully pointed foot.

All artists mold and shape their minds and bodies and also the space that confines their art. In this sense space is not only an empty stage but also a blank canvas, a block of marble, a lump of clay, a silent voice or musical instrument, or an unfinished verse. Every refining chisel stroke is a progressive step toward artistic transformation.

As aspiring artists persistently chip away to reveal perfection, they discover that many of those chips, which before seemed so important, were superfluous and needed to be discarded. They also find that other trifles, which previously seemed unimportant, are essential and need to be polished, so that the beauty of their work can shine.

The following chapters address many of the practical aspects of teaching classical ballet. Teachers who follow the guidelines in these chapters will organize and operate schools that contribute to the art of ballet and help students achieve their goals.

PART TWO *The Science of Teaching*

CHAPTER 6 *The Dance Studio*

---

*To excel the past we must not allow ourselves to lose
contact with it; on the contrary, we must feel it under
our feet because we have raised ourselves upon it.*

José Ortega y Gassett

Both students and parents should realize that the dance studio is a unique setting where dedication and self-discipline are the norm. It is not a playground or a gymnasium for after-school recreation, and it is *not* a child-care center.

Classical dance is one of our traditional art forms. To promote the art-workshop ambience, teachers and studio owners should maintain a stimulating decor that promotes artistic conduct. Objects displayed, colors chosen, and the arrangement of the office and waiting room should help create that ambience and be redolent of artistry and excellence in learning.

Let your young students and their parents know that classical ballet training should not be undertaken primarily as a means for girls to cultivate grace and poise or for young men to enhance athletic abilities, although it does have both of those benefits. Neither should dance be considered just one of many heterogeneous activities to fill in the week's agenda.

The desirability of having an artistic ambience in the studio pertains to all studio personnel as well. Everyone, including directors, teachers, accompanists, receptionists, even custodial help, should behave professionally, while at the same time being friendly and helpful toward parents, students, and visitors.

There are two main considerations in planning the layout of a studio, the division of space and the ambience you wish to convey. A division of space should include the following:

1. An office;
2. A parent/visitor waiting area;
3. A student lounge;
4. Dressing rooms; and
5. Classrooms.

OFFICE

Located near the main entry, the office should have a reception counter or desk. Immediately adjacent to the office should be an area where you can hold private conversations and make phone calls. There should also be a well-lit sitting area where visitors and guests can wait.

The office layout should be designed so that the receptionist can prevent unscreened visitors from wandering into areas of the studio reserved for students. In most cases, the office area should be out-of-bounds for students and parents.

WAITING AREA

Parents often escort their children to class. If the school is some distance from home or is not located in an area where there is nearby shopping, parents must wait. It is important that you provide a comfortable area for this purpose. Usually it is part of the office area or immediately adjacent to it. You need to provide suitable furniture and lighting, which help create an atmosphere that is not too spartan. You can provide current magazines, newspapers, and books to help pass the time. It is also opportune to schedule conferences and discuss other matters with parents while they are waiting.

LOUNGE

Here, students may study quietly, warm up before class, cool down and relax after class, have a nutritious snack or beverage, or just chitchat with their friends. It is best if this area is off limits to "civilians." Providing a lounge also helps to avoid congestion in doorways and hallways when classes are ending and students are going to and from the dressing rooms.

DRESSING ROOMS

Dressing rooms should be furnished with lockers to give students responsibility for organizing and protecting their belongings. In addition to toilets and washbasins, there should be a deep sink for janitorial use. If space allows, showers are a welcome addition. Benches or chairs are necessary to facilitate changing clothes and shoes. Two or three mirrors should be hung so makeup can be applied and hair combed. If carpeting is used, the best choice would be a durable indoor-outdoor type, as rosin and dirt get ground into noncommercial carpeting and make it difficult to clean. A vinyl floor-covering may be a more practical choice.

CLASSROOMS

Here many studio owners make the big mistake of skimping on space. You need a large studio where students can feel the spaciousness and expansiveness of their movements. Ideally, this space should have high ceilings and be approximately the size of a small stage. Fifty feet by thirty-five feet is a good minimum dimension. Small classrooms can inhibit students' movements and train them to "dance small." There should also be adequate observer seating arrangements, room for a piano and a sound system, and mirrors at least six feet tall across the front wall so that students can observe their full-length reflection.

In addition to the main studio, you should have at least one other studio, which should be totally separated from sound transfer. You can use the second studio for simultaneous classes, a warm-up room, or an extra rehearsal area. Constructing and maintaining extra classrooms may seem to be an unnecessary additional expense when establishing a new studio. However, they usually become extra income-earners for enterprising studio owners. Most successful owners eventually find that they need additional space as their activities expand.

Today every well-equipped studio requires a good quality sound system, including power amplifier, compact disc player, cassette tape player/recorder, variable-speed turntable, and loudspeakers. All of these should be top quality, made by manufacturers known for producing commercial-grade equipment. Because this system will receive hard use, equipment made primarily for home use is usually not durable enough. I have used a Technics Quartz Direct Drive Turntable, model SL-1200MK2, for over fifteen years without a single breakdown, except for stylus and cartridge replacements. It has a 16 percent range pitch (speed) control on a long slide, which makes it very convenient to vary tempo. This turntable is made for use by disc jockeys.

If you plan to use live accompaniment, I suggest you investigate one of the new professional digital pianos, such as the Yamaha. They have full-sized weighted keyboards that produce a sound close to that of a regular piano. They also have many "voices" that sound like strings, trumpets, organ, vocal chorus, and so forth, allowing an accomplished musician to compose and orchestrate. And, best of all, they never need tuning! Many digitals are portable enough that they could also provide live accompaniment during concerts or lecture-demonstrations. Most have their own self-contained stereo sound system, and they can also be wired directly through a remote sound system to give concert-hall volume.

It is becoming increasingly important for studios to include a good quality video camera and playback unit (VCR) in their inventory of equipment. Both VCR and TV monitor are now available in a single convenient unit. They have multiple uses in the classroom and especially during rehearsals and performances. Such visual learning aids help students see for themselves how they appear to others. The best technology now available for quality video equipment is 8 mm stereo with a minimum 8x zoom lens. A tripod is also useful.

It is extremely important that studio floors not be constructed directly over concrete subfloors or on subfloors resting directly on steel beams. Research has shown that one of the best arrangements is a sprung subfloor over which is laid either a special dance vinyl or a hardwood floor. There are several good sources for flooring material, but attention should first be given to how the subfloor is to be suspended above the concrete or beams.

One way is to underlay a minimum three-layer overlapping gridwork of crisscrossing wood strips (2" x 3" or 2" x 4" boards) set at intervals of approximately 16 inches, over which is installed either two layers of ½" plywood with the seams staggered or one layer of ¾" tongue-and-groove plywood.

Another floor is specially designed over heavy-duty springs at 12" to 16" intervals. These are sandwiched between 1" x 3" stripping attached to the subfloor and 2" x 3" or 2" x 4" boards running perpendicularly above. The plywood is then attached to these studs.

Other floor designs are available involving very dense, but resilient, foam blocks or sheets installed under the plywood. These and other designs help protect the dancers' legs and feet during classes and are essential for maintaining good health. Vinyl dancing surfaces, usually in six-foot wide sheets, are then applied to the plywood with adhesive for permanent installation, or with tape to keep the seams together for temporary installation. Traditionally, dance studio floors have been made of hardwood laid over a wooden subfloor, but the cost has become almost prohibitive.

Permanently installed barres are also important. It is not wise to use portable barres for everyday use. Regular use of portables should occur only in special situations, such as lecture-demonstrations or warm-up classes prior to performances.

Several years ago I had a welder fabricate a simple double-barre bracket that is attached directly to the wall and doesn't require any additional supports underneath. These barre brackets are bolted directly into the concrete block with lead anchors or into wood framing at 48-inch intervals. The barre material is ordinary 1½- or 1⅝-inch round pine handrail stock sanded smooth. Each bracket is made to hold the wood handrail in place by a simple wood screw which prevents it from turning in the students' hands. The double-barre design, which provides "over-under" barres approximately 9 inches apart, accommodates students of all ages and heights. And, since no under-supports are necessary, nothing gets in the way of students' legs or feet while they perform exercises toward the barre or with épaulement. These barres have survived many years in my studio without a single failure.

If necessary, heavy duty portable barres can be fabricated out of galvanized pipe and plumbing fittings. Made in this way, they can be easily disassembled for transportation to other locations. Six-foot lengths fit into small vans or station wagons, while eight-foot lengths can be transported in full-sized vans. Lightweight portables made out of aluminum, wood, or PVC pipe can also be purchased or fabricated. They are much easier to transport than the heavier galvanized pipe. However, they are less stable and are easily moved about by students during barre exercises.

FIGURE 1   *Dance floor underlayment*

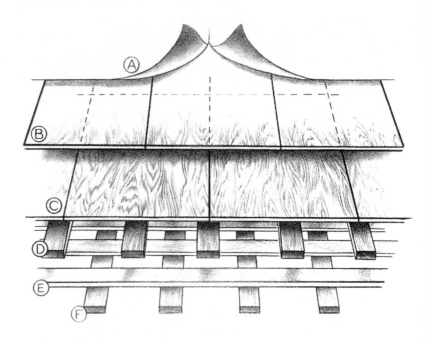

A. *Vinyl sheet dance flooring glued to plywood.*
B. *First layer of 4' x 8' x ½" plywood nailed or glued to second layer (joints must be offset).*
C. *Second layer of 4' x 8' x ½" plywood nailed or screwed to first layer of 2" x 3" boards.*
D. *First layer of 2" x 3" boards laid on 16" centers nailed or screwed to second layer.*
E. *Second layer of 2" x 3" boards laid on offset 16" centers nailed or screwed to third layer.*
F. *Third layer of 2" x 3" boards laid on offset 16" centers nailed or screwed into wood subfloor, or shot into concrete subfloor with bullet nails.*

FIGURE 2 *Sprung floor underlayment*

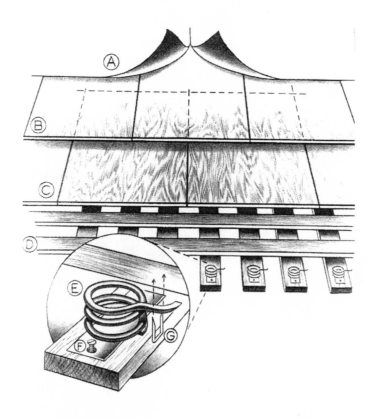

A. Vinyl sheet dance flooring glued to plywood.
B. First layer of 4' x 8' x ½" plywood nailed or screwed to second layer (joints must be offset).
C. Second layer of 4' x 8' x ½" plywood nailed or screwed to 2" x 3" boards.
D. 2" x 3" boards laid on 16" centers.
E. Spring (¼" diameter steel) shaped into 2½" (outside diameter) coil and welded to 5" x 1½" flange.
F. Flange screwed through 1" x 3" boards laid on 16" centers into wood subfloor, or shot into concrete subfloor with bullet nails.
G. Tail of spring (top ground flat) stapled onto 2" x 3" boards.

FIGURE 3   *Barre bracket*

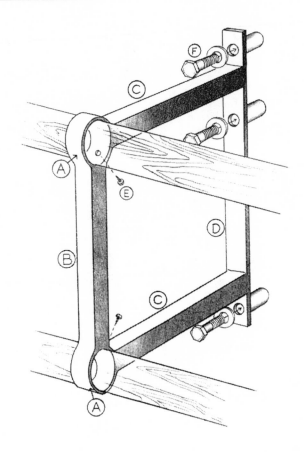

A. 1 " (wide) x 1 ⅝" (inside diameter) iron pipe sections drilled with ³⁄₁₆" hole for set screws.

B. 1 " (square) x 7" long iron tubing welded to (A).

C. 1 " (square) x 10" long iron tubing welded to (A).

D. 1 " iron flange x 14" long drilled with three ½" holes.

E. Set screw to keep wood handrail from moving.

F. ⅜"x 2" machine bolts with lock washers through flange into lead anchors set in holes drilled into concrete block wall, or ⅜"x 3" lag screws screwed into wall framing. Barre material is 1½" pine handrail stock. Upper barre is measured at 44" above the floor. Brackets are set 48" apart. After fabrication, brackets are primed and painted black.

DECOR GUIDELINES

The studio entrance, the office, and especially the classrooms should radiate an atmosphere of discipline and dedication. When students enter the building, everything they see and hear should encourage them to leave outside all mundane cares and distractions, such as term paper deadlines, exams, disagreements with family or friends, financial worries, and boyfriend/girlfriend problems. Everything they perceive inside the studio should remind them that they are there to learn to dance.

As students enter the classroom they should feel an atmosphere much like a theater's backstage area before a performance. Your responsibility as their teacher is to accustom students to adopt a demeanor of dignity and respect that is not merely artificial posturing during a lesson or a performance but will eventually become the normal way for responsive students to approach their daily work, an attitude indispensable to a budding performing artist.

While decorating the studio, avoid the temptation to pin up "baby-ballerina" pictures on the walls. Instead, obtain photographs from large-format classical dance books that depict academically accurate poses and positions. (Performance photographs of famous dancers are often not appropriate unless they illustrate the correctness of the intended pose.) Cut the photos out neatly and add appropriate captions. Then frame and hang them prominently, so that students will be constantly reminded how they should look while practicing their own exercises. In this way they can relate what they are doing in class to what they see in the photos. You might also consider hanging tasteful posters and original art in which ballet themes are beautifully depicted.

Place a bulletin board near the entrance to the lounge so that all students can see it as they pass by on their way to the dressing rooms and studios. Prominently display photos, news clippings, reviews, schedules, dance equipment supply sources, audition notices, and performance announcements. Attach cards and letters from your studio's graduates who are dancing professionally, teaching, choreographing, or running dance companies. In this way, your students become aware that, at *their* studio, it is normal to achieve high goals, to perform professionally, to travel abroad, and to be active in all aspects of the dance world. These ideas help you promote dance as a career to your promising students when they are ready to move into the public arena.

Ask students and parents to read the bulletin board frequently. Keep the display orderly, easy to read, and current.

CHAPTER 7 *Guidance*

Dancing . . . is no mere translation or
abstraction from life; it is life itself.

Havelock Ellis

Students study dance for many reasons. In a class of twenty students there might be an equal number of different reasons for studying. Each reason has its own level of validity. One person's reason might seem like another's folly, but each should be respected.

GUIDING CHILDREN

Children who study dance dream of stardom, of dancing *Swan Lake* and *The Nutcracker.* Their best friend "goes to ballet." Mom finds it convenient to drop them off when she goes shopping. Dad feels that they should have a variety of experiences. Their athletic coach recommends it.

Often students or parents shrink when they discover that studying dance is not merely a nice thing for young ladies to do. When serious formal classes begin, they suddenly feel daunted by the many formidable challenges they must confront.

In a majority of neighborhood ballet schools, young beginners typically attend class once a week. Some students would attend more often but are constrained by parents. Usually the reasons have to do with time or expense considerations. Sometimes parents restrict attendance because the regimen seems like an overly demanding schedule for their young children. When financial hardship is the sole preventive factor, teachers may choose to offer parents financial assistance.

However, the most common factor that seems to restrict attendance is that many parents simply do not wish to commit their own time—for driving, shopping for dance attire, or waiting during classes. Therefore, for example, reaching a three-times-per-week attendance schedule usually requires a certain amount of parental education.

With many children, after one or two years of dance lessons, the novelty begins to wear thin. By that time, even young students have discovered that, to dance well, there is much more involved than mere attendance. Unless strongly motivated and encouraged by their parents, it is likely that some children will drop out. This usually happens because unmotivated students never discover that the enjoyment of dancing is directly linked to the improvement one gains through dedication and hard work.

Some teachers get around this dropout problem through the excitement of the recital routine. Meanwhile, other students catch the ballet bug and ask their parents to increase the number of lessons per week, so they can speed up their progress or keep up with other fast-improving friends in class.

Another milestone is confronted when dance students enter high school. If they began their study at the optimal age of 8-10, they find themselves near the intermediate stage of proficiency and are well acquainted with hard work. But at this age there are unique demands from school and also from nature.

Nature confronts them with the challenges of puberty, which may result, among other things, in a change in their behavior toward their parents, their teacher, or their classmates. If not handled intelligently by the teacher, these biological changes can seriously interfere with their progress. I recommend that the reader interested in this subject search out sources for specific information on the psychology and physiology of adolescence.

New demands from high school begin with an accelerated intensity of academic expectations. Added to these are the pressures of wanting to be accepted by peers, become cheerleaders, join athletic teams, run for office, get a part-time job, or participate with friends in after-school and weekend activities. Also, teens may be cruelly judged by their peers when it is discovered they are dancers. The boys are often stereotyped as gay, and the girls as snobbish.

And there is the all-important dating game, which has its tentative beginnings in junior high school. For many adolescents this activity becomes the be-all and end-all of everyday life. To many young dancers' great surprise, it often turns out that no one is more jealous of their hours spent at the ballet studio than the new boyfriend or girlfriend. Dance teachers can anticipate possible changes in attendance, in attitude and demeanor, and in ability to concentrate on the work in class. Sometimes, unless these students are strongly motivated to continue, they abandon their dreams and leave their dance studies. This happens to the talented as well as the plodders.

COLLEGE OR CAREER?

Those who survive the challenges of the high school freshman milestone and persist with their dance training are eventually confronted by another difficult decision. Having by now achieved an advanced level of study, many serious ballet students are told by parents and high school counselors that they must now "get serious" about their futures. They are expected to make decisions about applying for acceptance to college and also about other nondance-related career choices.

Continuing their education in a college or university will make it difficult for serious students to continue dance training at the professional level. The vast majority of institutions of higher learning lack a truly professional curriculum in dance. There are few exceptions.

Many high school counselors and educators do not consider the years spent studying dance to be a major factor in determining a career. They tend to guide the student away from this area of interest toward more prosaic directions, where academic achievement directly equates with job placement and success. For many parents and school administrators dance is considered an after-school activity.

A dedicated student who is considering dance as a possible career needs to be exposed to as much of the professional dance world as possible. Thoughtful dance teachers can provide assistance in several ways. Excursions to nearby performances of professional dance companies can be arranged. Be sure to also include opera, symphony, theater, and museums.

Arrange for your best preprofessional advanced students to take company classes with visiting companies and to observe rehearsals. Some touring companies allow dancers to audition during company classes while on the road. Invite touring companies to hold their classes or rehearsals in your studio. Host a reception in honor of the visiting company. Ask the company to send someone to teach a master class in your studio, preferably the company ballet master or artistic director.

You can show videotapes and movies of dance. Ask students for comments on what they observe. Keep the atmosphere casual, but conduct the event in a professional manner.

High school seniors and their parents need the objective counsel of a knowledgeable and clear-thinking dance teacher. Should they go to an academic college? Or a college with a dance department? Are they ready to audition for a professional company? Are they big or small company material? Should they consider dancing in Europe or Latin America? Should they consider accepting a trainee or apprentice position with a company? Are they talented enough to prepare for national or international competitions? All these questions require thoughtful answers tailored to the individual student's level of talent and interest.

What about those hard-working students who have the requisite desire and parental support but are only marginally talented or truly not professional dance material? Students who wish to pursue a dance career in spite of the negatives must be told about the realities of the world of professional dance. If they have difficulty accepting your counsel, send them to auditions so they can see for themselves what the competition is like and also feel the level of intensity and the demand for instant competence, without excuses. Such raw experience may convince them more readily than your dissuasive words. I must report, however, that there are many examples of highly committed students who have found a niche in the professional world of dance, despite a bare modicum of talent.

Ask students who wish to apply to colleges as dance majors to show you copies of the prospective schools' dance curricula. Review the material with them. Direct them to the good points and deficiencies of the curriculum. Explain that such courses are not always designed to open avenues for professional dancing careers. My experience has shown that there are very few dance colleges that have courses designed to groom competent professionals, let alone help talented artists achieve high goals.

Some college dance departments are headed by academic personnel who have little or no professional background in the field. Others offer little more than a dancercize adjunct to a physical education department. Some may be staffed by former professional dancers. However, it must be understood that mere possession of a college degree or a teaching certificate, or even spending years on the stage, do not, per se, comprise qualification for teaching dance, especially at the professional level.

A potentially good college or university dance program should be administered by a dean or department head who has a professional dance background—as should the faculty. All should have backgrounds in learning teaching skills from master-teachers. Classes should be graded according to ability. Placement should not be determined solely by one's age or grade in school.

In determining the quality of a college dance program, some important questions need to be asked. What is the percentage of graduates who find meaningful work in professional companies or in alternate related professions? If one is choosing a teaching emphasis, what are the qualifications of the faculty? And, most importantly, *who has taught them how to teach?* Are there performing opportunities? How many per year? What are the studio facilities like? Is there a daily technique lesson? Pointe? Variations? Partnering? Character-Ethnic? Modern? Jazz?

Some graduating high school dance students are prime candidates for well-designed college dance programs. I refer to those who clearly have no possibility of succeeding as professional dancers, but who, because of a combination of academic skills, their love for the art, and their many years of dance training, possess many requisites to succeed in a related, but nonperforming aspect, of the performing arts.

Examples of related careers might include publicist, business manager, costume designer, booking agent, talent scout, physical therapist, dance equipment salesperson, dance critic, set designer, lighting director, stage manager, actor, producer, fund-raiser, company executive director, attorney specializing in theatrical cases, and in exceptional cases where there is a background of professional-caliber training and talent, dance teacher or choreographer.

There is a need for knowledgeable arts support personnel who understand the special needs of dancers, ballet masters, and choreographers. If dance students who opt for college programs could be guided in these directions, they could provide an important service to the art by helping to stabilize the business and administrative side of dance.

I recently heard that out of the thousands of college basketball players in any given year only twenty-five to thirty will ever make it to a professional team, and many of them will just sit on the bench. The percentages are probably similar for ballet dancers. Those few high school juniors and seniors who have a realistic chance of becoming professional dancers are at the most challenging time of their lives. They must dare to be judged objectively and subjectively, and in some cases, ruthlessly by people who do not really care how much they love to dance. They must prove to harsh critics that they possess the skills and artistry required to dance professionally.

At this stage of development, students trying to break into the professional side of the art must be given parental support and encouragement, especially during the emotionally trying moments of failure at competitions and auditions. Without support at this time they may lose the self-confidence needed to continue their struggle. It is also important for young hopefuls to realize that choices made by company directors are often whimsical and based purely upon personal taste rather than an objective evaluation of the prospect's potential.

If you are convinced that your students are ready for the audition circuit, remind them that the people who do the hiring are scouting for prospective dancers at auditions, at competitions, at local performances, and even during visitations to dance studios. The more determinedly your students persist, and the more broadly they expose themselves, the sooner their job will materialize.

Make sure that your students understand they are attempting to achieve something that is attained by only a handful of special people. It is both a privilege and a great responsibility to be a professional dancer. It is much more than just the fulfillment of an individual's dream. The perpetuation of the art depends on the seriousness and dedication that students put into their work. There are unique demands and rewards awaiting those who succeed. For a person to share emotions and inspirations and to stand alone on a stage before thousands of expectant fellow human beings is a unique experience that cannot be purchased at any price.

The expression of art is about humanity aspiring to something better. The artist's responsibility is to show the audience an acutely focused realization that life is truly an exciting adventure. A performer's efforts are judged while standing exposed onstage—naked, as it were. The audience must decide if a performance merits a polite pitter-patter of hands, or if a great performance has inspired bravos and critical acclaim. Such special experiences are surely among the most unique communications available to mankind.

WHEN TO START?

In the state schools of the former Soviet Union, serious formal training begins between the ages of nine and ten. By then, children's bodies and minds have developed sufficiently to be able to benefit from the discipline required. Nine-year-olds' muscles are far stronger and better coordinated than most seven- and eight-year-olds. And they are emotionally more ready to go to work.

However, it is common in the United States to see beginning students start as young as three or four years of age. It should be obvious that the older students' intellect, attention span, physical strength, and capacity for self-discipline are far in advance of their younger counterparts. And older beginners can grasp the importance of the work they are attempting. Most very young students require an inordinate amount of repetitive instruction relating to the basics and become disinterested when called upon to spend the extra time necessary to perfect details.

While it is virtually impossible to teach a strict curriculum of classical ballet to the very young, some teachers develop preballet courses for children aged five through seven or eight. These lessons are somewhat shorter, and much less demanding than regular beginning ballet classes. Preballet or creative movement lessons should contain few, if any, academic ballet exercises. They should concentrate more on coordinating simple movements with music by employing such devices as improvising games that involve walking, skipping, marching, and clapping to a variety of musical rhythms. Teachers of these classes might integrate very simple ballet ingredients into these games, without insisting on precise muscle control, turnout, or the basic stance (TBS).

Many teachers of preballet age children have discovered that their students are able to learn French ballet terms with amazing alacrity. In this way teachers can make preballet curricula more beneficial to these young children.

Knowledgeable teachers who plan well can introduce a modified ballet curriculum to eight-year-olds. However, a class of fifteen eight-year-olds will progress relatively slowly, as many children at that age are still somewhat physically uncoordinated and find it difficult to focus attention for long periods of time. Nevertheless, you can expect better results than with children who are younger. Most eight-year-olds can cope with a ninety-minute lesson if the teacher blends perspicacity with patience.

WHEN TO BEGIN POINTE?

In the state schools of the former Soviet Union, where carefully selected nine- to ten-year-olds study every day, children in the first class begin simple pointe exercises in the second semester, toward the end of the year. Their exercises are carefully supervised and are done facing the barre while holding on with both hands. It is important to reiterate that these first-year students are talented children with well-formed bodies and feet, whose muscles have been strengthened through their regimen of daily lessons over a period of several months.

In contrast, most teachers in the West consider themselves very fortunate to have more than two or three talented beginning students. And how many of our beginners take daily lessons? Because of this situation, it is necessary to modify our pointe curriculum by working slowly for a longer period of time while facing the barre and covering less material.

Separate pointe lessons, even at the advanced level, are not recommended. Instead, it is far more productive to give pointe for fifteen to twenty minutes at the end of the students' regular ballet lesson several times a week. This system accustoms students to the rigors (and discomfort) of pointe work and prepares them to dance later for long hours in pointe shoes as professionals.

In the West it has become common for dancers to wear pointe shoes during regular technique lessons, even in company classes. Many company directors and ballet masters even require it. This device is usually employed as a therapeutic remedy for weak ankles and feet. The weakness could be easily dealt with if teachers understood the importance of regular work on demi-pointe in their daily lessons. A well-designed technique lesson that challenges the students to the maximum cannot be danced in pointe shoes. The difficulties presented by using these special shoes make it nearly impossible to get the most out of the exercises that comprise a well-planned lesson. Master-teachers know how to design lessons that contain many strength-building ingredients that prepare girls for pointe later on.

You can modify a pointe curriculum by postponing putting students on pointe until you are certain their ankles and feet are strong. This might mean waiting until the third year of study for students who do not attend class more than twice a week. And for students who come only once a week, you should discourage pointe work altogether. These students will never develop the strength to use pointe shoes properly and safely.

Teachers must also make decisions about students with physical problems, such as the chronically overweight; severe scoliosis of the back; flat feet (no discernible arch); unusually bowed legs or knees that cannot straighten; crossed or bent toes or toes of unequal length; toes with ingrown nails, corns, and so forth; crookedly healed broken toes, feet, or ankle bones; or inflexible ankle joints.

In most cases, unless students are able to correct such deficiencies through outside therapy (keeping in mind that some of the above problems are not correctable), they have little chance of achieving even the advanced-amateur level of proficiency in classical dance. Dancing professionally in a classical company is probably out of the question. It is an unjustifiable risk for a teacher to teach pointe to students with serious disabilities. The possibility of injury—already high with completely healthy students—is greatly increased with such problems. It may be wise to steer such students, who deeply love to dance, toward another dance form, such as modern, tap, or jazz. Of course, one can enjoy the study of classical dance without dancing on pointe.

Another question that often arises concerns students who have hyperextended joints (joints that bend past the point of alignment when straightened) and students with overly arched insteps. These students must be given the strictest attention during their formative years of training. They must be taught how to keep their legs straight without pressing back or rolling over into the joints. It is very important that teachers insist that these students maintain correct alignment and muscular control of the knees and feet at all times, especially while dancing on pointe. The thigh and lower leg must be kept vertically aligned with the knee, and the knee joint must be straight and firm and must not be allowed to push back (lock) into the joint. Active thigh muscles help hold the knee in place.

Students fortunate enough to have beautifully arched feet often need extra foot-strengthening exercises. Additional relevés on demi-pointe will help them build the strength to dance safely on pointe and retain their natural gift. Practicing relevés on both legs and on one leg, both with and without plié, as part of each day's barre and center exercises, helps to achieve this end.

When students begin wearing pointe shoes, make sure they use the strength of their legs, ankles, and feet to stand on pointe. They must not depend on the shoe's arch support and box to support their weight. They must not allow their weight to settle into the shoe. This is potentially danger-

FIGURE 4   *Hyperextended knees*

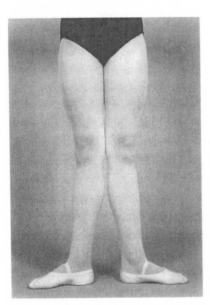 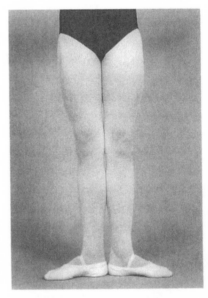

Hyperextended knees: knees touching,
while feet are separated in first position.

Hyperextension corrected: knees
and feet are touching in first position.

ous, because the misalignment of the leg caused by hyperextended knee joints and high arches of the feet sends the body's weight into the shoe instead of through the leg and foot. This problem can quickly break down the built-in support of the shoes, requiring premature replacement of these extremely expensive shoes.

Watch out for ankle pronation! While children are very young, they can (and often do) easily roll their ankles inward or outward, placing great stress on ankle bones and knees. If allowed to continue, this practice can be devastating to the ankle joint. In time pronation may overstretch the ankle tendons so that pointe work is rendered unsafe. In addition, pronation can lead to bunions in the large joint of the big toe. To counteract this problem, the leg must remain vertically aligned, with the foot stretching straight ahead, neither bending inwards nor outwards. Teachers should strongly emphasize this correct method of stretching the feet to avoid injuries.

FIGURE 5   *Highly arched foot*

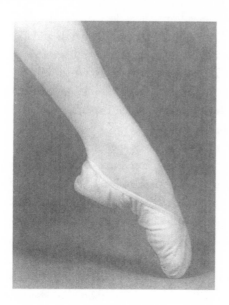

Beginning students should purchase lightweight pointe shoes, avoiding styles made with extra-heavy shanks and boxes or stiffened heavy-fabric shoes. Urge your students to try several different brands over a period of time, until they find the one that feels best for them. Remind students and parents that pointe shoes should never be purchased oversized "to allow room to grow in." And they should always be fitted by someone who has been properly trained.

Some studio owners have found it advantageous (and profitable) to have ballet shoe concessions inside the studio. These might be operated by an interested parent, a parents' club, a representative from a local dance-supplies store, a teacher, or a retired dancer who knows what dancers' feet need. Everyone benefits from such an arrangement as long as dancers' interests, not income production, are paramount.

The matter of correctly fitted shoes is an important issue. As mentioned before, pointe shoe fitting should be done by a trained person who can evaluate needs and prescribe the best shoe to wear. Students can be easily confused by the many choices available. Not only do manufacturers make a variety of different styles of shoes, but each style is made with different shaped boxes, vamps, and insole strengths. They come in whole and half sizes and in different widths. Some are made quite durable and survive several pointe lessons and rehearsals, while others have a short life and are best used for performance only. Shoes can be made to last a bit longer by darning the pointes and coating them with hardening agents. Experienced dancers learn techniques to give pointe shoes extra life.

Often, within a manufacturer's specific shoe style, there are several individual cobblers (shoe makers). Sometimes cobblers will make their particular shoes slightly different from their colleagues'. When you find a maker whose shoes consistently fit comfortably, it is best to stick with that maker. Finally, it is possible to special-order shoes for feet that are particularly sensitive or unusually shaped. Naturally, such shoes will cost more than those purchased off the shelf.

Teachers should budget sufficient class time to include one or more brief lessons on how to attach elastic and ribbons to the shoes, and how to tie ribbons properly. A dancer whose ribbons unravel and drawstrings hang out, or whose shoes constantly slip off the heels, is a careless dancer. Part of the

FIGURE 6   *Pronation and supination of the foot*

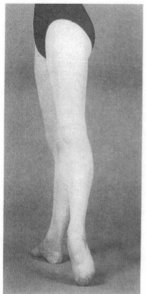 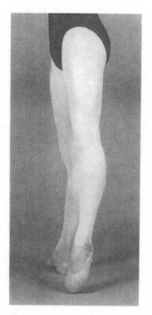 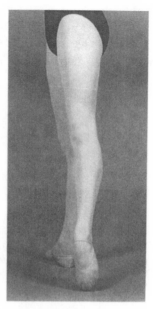

Pronation (eversion).   Supination (inversion).   Foot correctly stretched.

dancer's stage craft is knowing how to prepare and wear the essential para-phernalia. If a teacher detects that students are having trouble with their elas-tic and ribbons, appoint some advanced students to take the slow learners and new students aside, outside of class, and work with them until they have mastered it.

BABY BALLERINAS

The famous modern dance pioneer Isadora Duncan once said, "Love is the vision of the soul when it is permitted to gaze upon immortal beauty."

In many of today's professional dance companies there seems to be an unprecedented infatuation with youth. In the print media, many American companies are referred to as young companies. In many instances, this does not refer to the age of the company but to the average age of the company's

FIGURE 7   *How to tie pointe shoe ribbons*

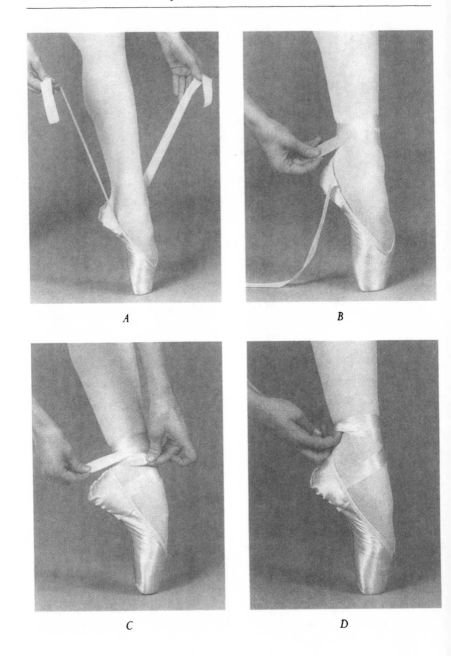

A

B

C

D

dancers. The corps de ballet of many ballet companies today are primarily staffed by teenagers. This phenomenon also includes, on occasion, soloists and even principal dancers.

This phenomenon is especially prevalent in competitive gymnastics, where very young and physically immature children have enormous pressures placed on them by coaches who press young bodies far beyond safe limits. The demanding regimen of competitive gymnastics causes participants' musculature to develop far ahead of their bone development. The extraordinarily developed muscles of young gymnasts cause participants to believe that their bodies can be stressed to the extreme. However, their bones are still in a developmental stage and cannot keep pace with the demands placed upon the muscles. This is a subject for orthopedic specialists.

Injuries are commonplace in young gymnasts. Many teenagers who are serious about competition undergo operations to repair damage to cartilage and ligaments and are also treated for stress fractures. Added to these pressures are emotional and psychological stresses stemming from mind-games imposed by some coaches and teachers, who only want to work with winners.

These psychological tricks combine extremes of loving care with aloof indifference. It is no wonder that gymnasts have very short careers. Their bodies and minds are so stressed out by the time they are eighteen years old that they cannot continue. This is a phenomenon that seems to have begun with the famous Soviet gymnast Olga Korbut.

Inexperienced and immature dancers must also be very careful to work with teachers who help them develop in a healthy and natural way. Very young dancers who are pushed prematurely to enter professional companies are ill-equipped for the demands of the work. Certainly, they have talent. Certainly, they can follow direction and be coached. But they have barely begun to live and lack life experiences and maturity to call upon. Most dancers who attempt this mistaken approach fail to reach their promised potential and fade into obscurity while still very young.

Some well-known choreographers have made dance-world headlines by "discovering" very young dancers and making them instant stars. But the effect on the minds of most of these young dancers has been devastating. An apt analogy would be the folly of placing a high school "superstar" athlete directly onto the starting lineup of a professional basketball or football team, depriving him of the learning experiences and necessary maturation that only come with time. Young dancers learn stagecraft and artistry through the apprenticeship of well-performed peripheral roles, graduating through merit and small successes into ever greater journeyman responsibilities of increasingly important supporting roles.

The awesome pressures and responsibilities of stardom challenge even the most secure adults. It is not realistic to expect an inexperienced young person, who has barely departed the insulated life of school and family, to be able to deal wisely with these extraordinary burdens. Who is willing to take responsibility for the tragedy of young artists turning to drugs, alcohol, promiscuous sex, emotional mood swings, even suicide, that could result from a premature fishbowl existence? Is the discovering director or choreographer to blame? Or the parent who allowed (or pushed) the child? Or the teacher who remained silent while the student was being exploited? Or audiences who eagerly pay to see these young phenomena?

Some *very* gifted dancers (and their parents) have allowed themselves to be pressured into this situation. Rising young stars inevitably become the target of jealous older dancers' criticism and envy, and also fair game for acerbic dance critics. My experience is that most teenagers—even those who seem mature for their years—should not be tempted by the challenge of coping with these pressures. Prematurely embarking on a promising career is shortsighted. History has given us many examples of tragic endings stemming from this problem.

In the former Soviet Union, exceptionally talented dancers are given special care. To avoid such premature pressures, especially gifted young dancers may be invited to join a special "Class of Perfection," where their technique and artistic abilities are honed and refined. These young dancers are carefully groomed for future leading positions and are guided and nurtured by senior or retired dancers who are assigned to be their coaches and mentors. These elder artists help prepare their protégés for the roles assigned to them, both technically and with their artistic interpretations. Such close associations often last for several years.

Once, while touring the Soviet Union, I saw a performance of *Giselle* given in Moscow's Bolshoi Theatre. In this performance a young soloist was dancing the principal role for the first time. I was told that she had been receiving individual coaching on her role for *one year!* Her partner, one of the most experienced leading male dancers in the company, provided superlative support. In the wings and in special boxes assigned to the company staff were her teachers, her coach, other dancer-friends, and ballet masters. The performance was close to perfection, leaving hardly anything to criticism. She was obviously extremely well prepared. Her artistic interpretation was exceptional, and her technique impeccable. She received a well-deserved standing ovation and many curtain calls and flowers. It was a deeply moving experience and says a great deal about how serious Russian artists are about their work.

This talented young dancer had already spent several years as a corps member and soloist performing roles of steadily increasing responsibility. It was a combination of all these elements of maturation and nurturing that made it possible for her to achieve such heights in her first performance of such an important role.

Talented young dancers need to be wisely and carefully groomed for stardom. Their time comes soon enough. The primary role of their elders is to prepare them to cope with all of the challenges that accompany these experiences. Let's not rush our charges into the unforgiving maw of center stage spotlight. Rather, let's protect them from youthful ambition's impetuousness.

GUIDING ADULTS

Every year thousands of adults begin exploring experiences associated with dance. Some do so with discipline and focused purpose, but the majority begin with a tentative and casual approach. How should teachers respond to adults who are past the optimal starting age for serious study?

There are those who believe dance to be one of the most arduous of all physical endeavors. To be sure, it takes a certain amount of courage to overcome the intimidation of its daunting challenges. If studying dance is a first-time experience, adults need to be reassured that the reticence they feel is normal and that beginners at every age level go through these same pangs of discomfort and embarrassment.

There are many reasons for adults beginning such a demanding regimen. Each has its own validity. My experience has shown that some beginning adult students dreamed of becoming dancers when younger but were unable to study for various reasons. Other adults return to ballet after experiencing previous dance training as youngsters. Some have friends who are dancing. Some want to go beyond the rote athleticism of aerobics and fitness-center "dancercize" routines to a physical activity that will help them keep in shape. Others are athletically inclined and want to explore dance as a means of improving their skills in other areas of interest.

Some adults have had their interest piqued by a movie, a video, a book, a TV program, or a live concert. Some enjoy the feeling of moving their bodies to music. Others come for the social intercourse. Some students, encouraged by their teachers, may come to ballet from other theater arts backgrounds to learn how to move more gracefully onstage.

Once enrolled, teachers are faced with fitting them into an appropriate class. If the studio has a fairly small number of students and a limited number of classes, it may be difficult to find a place for new adult beginners, unless a new class is forming. It is not a good idea to combine children younger than thirteen with adults. Each age group tends to intimidate the other. The above stated reasons for adult ballet study are usually quite different from those that motivate younger students. It should also be clear that the learning pace of a thirty-year-old beginner is quite different from that of a ten-year-old. Experienced teachers find that the instructional approach between children's and adult classes needs to be quite different.

Since many adults prefer morning or evening classes, establishing a schedule for adult groups usually does not present a problem. However, if adult beginner demands become so great that you begin to experience scheduling conflicts, you may need to move your studio to larger facilities or build an addition onto your existing studio. If you have an exceptionally large studio, consider subdividing the existing space. Maybe you could rent or purchase the building next door or the floor above.

With the above changes you will need to advertise vigorously and promote these classes to cover the increased expenses. However, the extra income derived from additional classes usually justifies the expense. You will also find that the networking process of adding these classes has far-reaching effects. Satisfied adult students are your most avid goodwill ambassadors. The good word spread around your community by happy adult students is a valuable asset. And don't forget that your adult students' own children are potential enrollees, along with their friends who might also wish to enroll or who have children.

Lessons for adults should be constructed along the same progressive lines as for children. However, there is an extremely wide range of mental acuity, physical flexibility, and muscular strength in adults. This means that while most adults are able to move at a faster pace than eight- to ten-year-olds, some adults will need to move more slowly. It takes special thought and preparation to devise a curriculum that is both satisfying and challenging for older students.

Many adults find it tedious to spend a great deal of class time on explanations and detailed technical analysis. Since they are there to dance, they want to move at a faster pace. But teachers need to make clear to all students the importance of being well grounded in all the fundamentals. Adults must understand that this can only be done methodically and progressively. The proper blending of mental and physical education in dance requires that nothing be skipped over lightly. This is not just because of tradition, but for the students' safety, since in classical dance bodies move in ways very different from what most people consider normal.

It is up to each teacher to meet the aforementioned dance curriculum requirements while keeping the atmosphere congenial. The teacher needs to find ways to give self-conscious adults corrections without embarrassing them. Be sure to have a sense of humor. And the clever teacher will always prepare a simple, dancey combination at the end of every lesson, so that the students feel they are really dancing.

An often overlooked aspect of adult ballet study is that the students, even if they progress no further than the beginner or intermediate levels, become better informed and discriminating audiences. Their enthusiasm for dance can be infectious to their spouses, friends, and business associates. They also comprise the nucleus of supporters of professional dance companies as board members and volunteers. Enthusiastic adult students are the art's best word-of-mouth advertisers. In addition to providing personal financial support, many working adults might also have potentially important corporate and business connections. Their support, whether substantial or minimal, helps keep the art alive and well. In sum, treat *all* your students with respect and courtesy. They will sense your goodwill and usually respond accordingly.

A final thought—sometimes it is necessary to give attention to important details other than the beauties of dance. In the area of safety, for example, there is an increasing body of legal precedent holding commercial athletics-related businesses responsible for injuries experienced by their clientele. These injuries include such areas as circulation complications, heart attacks, joint and bone problems, back problems, and strained and sprained muscles and ligaments.

We all know the skyrocketing costs of litigation. Even defendants who win cases are usually out-of-pocket many thousands of dollars and many hours of valuable time. You might wish to consider a policy of requiring a "waiver of liability" form that is valid in your state's legal system.

THE DANCER'S BODY

> *Life rushes from within, not from without. There is*
> *no work of art so big or so beautiful that it was not*
> *all once contained in some youthful body.*
>
> Willa Cather

In recent years, a voguish female body type has become the norm in classical dance. Far from emulating the classical Greek ideal, so much admired and depicted over the centuries by painters such as Degas and sculptors such as Rodin, this new norm has narrowed the range of acceptable body types for dance. In effect, this norm has redefined what is meant by the term *feminine beauty*.

As students of art history know, widely divergent definition and periodic redefining of feminine beauty have been going on for centuries, evolving through many socially acceptable definitions, some of which are the mysterious beauty epitomized by Egyptian Queen Nefertiti; the abundant beauty of Raphael and Titian; the powerful beauty of the Scandinavian Valkyrie; the concealed beauty of Arabian concubines; the modest beauty of oriental femininity; the waist-laced, bosom-enhanced beauty of the European court; the bawdy beauty of the French can-can dancer; the glamorous beauty of the rich and famous; the athletic beauty of bodybuilders; and, finally, the gaunt beauty of high-fashion models and late-twentieth-century classical ballet dancers.

Historically, each of the above has been reflected in the dance style of the culture it sprang from. Dance, like most arts, tends to reflect current tastes rather than set trends; therefore, dancers are subject to whatever ideals of beauty are in vogue at the time. Many dance professionals feel the gaunt beauty ideal of female dancers of the present generation has been detrimental to those who feel compelled to conform to it.

The new female-dancer look is typified by one who is comparatively tall, long-limbed, pale-skinned, and long-necked. She has a small head with delicate but prominent facial features. And she has boyish hips and an unobtrusive bust. These are the physical features of today's female dancer who, paradoxically, is supposed to combine both femininity and sexlessness.

This paradox correlates with the androgynous type that has, in recent years, become increasingly more prevalent in the fields of clothing fashion, women's athletics, and popular rock and punk music. Some advocates tout the streamlined appearance this physique gives to dancers onstage, especially when dancers in a group are wearing the same leotard or unitard.

This look became popular during the Balanchine years at the New York City Ballet Company. No doubt he preferred this look because many of the ballets he choreographed in the early years were danced without scenery or elaborate costumes. And, of course, Balanchine's choreography placed strong emphasis on the legs and feet, which are more easily seen without costume. The body type that accompanies the legs and feet he admired is usually associated with a slender build.

Today, as Balanchine's ballets are performed more and more by other companies, this new look has become universally accepted, influencing public taste in the art all over the world. This attitude continues to pervade the dance scene through many of Balanchine's disciples, who have, since his death, become directors of ballet companies. The look has become all-important, often relegating essential artistic qualities to the background. I hope this unfortunate situation is not permanent.

There is a considerable price exacted to achieve this new look, especially when it is not one's natural body type. The androgynous appearance is often accompanied by abnormal physical development and sexual dysfunction. There are some who are born naturally with this body type. However, as we know, the female body usually develops differently. To achieve this look, many female dancers suffer abnormal regimens involving experimentation with radical dieting that often results in malnutrition and anorexia or bulimia. Obsessive preoccupation with their appearance is commonplace.

There is also the danger of drug dependency. Sometimes unnecessary cosmetic surgery is employed. There are bouts of depression leading to emotional distress. And dancers may also suffer with chronic injury and constant attention by doctors, chiropractors, and physical therapists.

The above disorders demonstrate that the look is often achieved at great expense, resulting in tragic losses to the art. For example, it is commonplace for many companies to be plagued by a sizable roster of continually injured dancers. Performances are seriously compromised (even occasionally canceled) due to last minute cast changes. Of course, such problems exist in other performing arts, but not to the extent they do in dance. Last-minute cancellations and program changes are particularly disgruntling to audiences. And they also force unprepared dancers into last-minute substitutions, cheating audiences of their expectations.

Many gifted dancers are denied the opportunity to show their talents and develop their artistry because they do not have the look. Can one imagine the world of dance without the unique contributions of Galina Ulanova, Nora Kaye, Alicia Alonso, Martha Graham, Andre Eglevsky, Martine van Hamel, Cynthia Gregory, Mikhail Baryshnikov, Vaslav Nijinsky, and a host of other great artists who did not possess the look? It is interesting to note that most, if not all, of the above artists might never have passed the infamous body check, which is now part of many auditions.

Two such experiences point out the absurdity of the situation. I was present at an important New York audition where more than half of the dancers were eliminated before the first dance combination was given because they did not have the brown eyes that the choreographer was seeking. On another occasion, an outstanding dancer I knew was cut during an audition following a walk across the floor, before being allowed to dance a single step. A few months later she went on to win an important international competition and later became a soloist in a major company.

THE STUDENT-TEACHER RELATIONSHIP

With the exception of performance warm-ups, the ballet lesson should provide a learning opportunity for all students in attendance, whether young beginners or accomplished professionals. For this to happen teachers must come to each lesson prepared, and students must approach the lesson in a frame of mind conducive to learning. Although this seems obvious, it is not always the case.

For the teaching-learning process to be most beneficial, a rapport between teachers and students must develop. Students must learn to trust their teachers, to accept everything the teacher says as the truth. Students should be like sponges, soaking up all the knowledge and information their teachers give them. Young students usually have no trouble accepting such a relationship. When students look up to and respect their teachers, the entire experience is rewarding and fruitful.

However, as students mature, hitherto productive student-teacher relationships may be affected. Attitudes and expectations change. Focus shifts, and discipline can be affected by a variety of extraneous influences. Teachers must be aware of such changes. Most of them can be handled with consideration.

One of the most destructive influences imposed upon the student-teacher relationship is loss of respect. When a student loses respect, for whatever reason, real or imagined, the learning process generally grinds to a halt. The student begins to question the teacher's credibility, which sometimes happens as a result of something the teacher does or says.

Students may feel that the teacher is showing favoritism toward others, or that they are being treated indifferently. In other instances the students may begin to feel that they know more than their teacher. This sometimes happens after students have visited another school, particularly when the visit has been to a well-known ballet center where they have taken classes with a famous teacher. Attitudes can also change after returning home from a summer course offered by a professional company, or if a student has successfully competed in a national or international competition.

All too often impressionable young students are overly influenced by the atmosphere of crowded classrooms containing "name" professionals and the special attention they may receive from teachers and other dancers in the class. Only well-grounded students are able to resist the distracting influences of such encounters and realize that they still have much to learn. Students who are still learning need to come down to earth after the excitement of their experience and get back to work.

There is another reason for the breakdown of the student-teacher relationship. Sometimes advanced students and professional dancers elect to use the daily lesson much like someone attending a fitness center for a personal workout. With this self-centered attitude dancers use the lesson for personal reasons and are not interested in, or receptive to, instruction from the teacher. In such cases the lesson ceases to be a learning experience. It becomes just a stay-in-shape workout or an opportunity for these dancers to work on specific things of their own. Unfortunately, experienced dancers fall into this trap.

Almost without exception, most finished dancers like to work on the things they do best. If left to their own devices they avoid confronting their weaknesses. They may even resist a teacher's attempt to help them, which is often the case when a famous dancer visits a teacher's class. With master-teachers, who are quite secure within themselves, this usually does not present a problem. However, insecure teachers might be intimidated by the dancer's indifferent attitude toward their methods. For dancers who attempt to impose their will in this way, learning ceases. During the lesson everyone in attendance is a student once again and should allow the learning process to continue.

Classes for even the most accomplished professional dancers should be challenging and demanding. Otherwise, technical weaknesses will begin to invade. If company classes were always more demanding than the challenges dancers face during their performances, there would be far fewer work-related injuries and much greater longevity.

It is up to teachers to decide whether or not they are willing to allow such breakdowns in their classes. Regardless of the reason for the breakdown of the student-teacher relationship, the resulting negative atmosphere stifles the learning process and should not be tolerated.

CHAPTER 8

The Lesson

When purest feeling forms the line
It sends a slave upon the stage
The art is left to wait behind
For here do breathe the earth and fate.

Boris Pasternak

The classical ballet lesson is based upon organization and planning. Teachers and students should be fully prepared for the experience—teachers with their lesson plan—students alert, focused, and eager to learn. Although daily lessons are necessary for students to achieve high goals as future dancers and for professional dancers to maintain peak technical form, they must never be allowed to deteriorate into rote routines. Teachers play an active part in providing an atmosphere that is conducive to this unique learning experience.

Before a lesson begins, students should assemble in the classroom at the barre, spacing themselves so each has adequate room to work. This basic preparation seems obvious; however, all too often, one sees students lounging around outside the classroom or gathered in groups along the barre, while they wait for the lesson to begin. I feel that it promotes a better working frame of mind if students learn the discipline of being in the classroom, more or less near their chosen place at the barre, before the teacher enters. This promotes promptness and demonstrates a ready attitude on the student's part.

A number of teachers have reported good results from adopting the custom of beginning the lesson by having their students perform a révérence (bow) in unison directed toward their teacher. This prelude to the lesson is a respectful greeting, accompanied by musical cues, as the students stand near their positions at the barre. This procedure accomplishes two ends. It accustoms the students to adopt a theatrical mind-set, and it helps direct their minds to the purpose for being there, before the first exercise begins.

During the barre exercises, as well as during the center and allegro sections of the lesson, insist on clean beginnings and controlled endings. Students should cultivate an attitude of eager readiness by mentally preparing to execute correctly *every detail* of barre work, *every detail* of center work, and *every detail* of allegro. Whenever students begin an exercise in a sloppy or hesitant manner, falter while executing a combination, or end an exercise weakly, the teacher must insist that the students pull themselves together and finish with authority. By developing this habit students learn that it is not a disgrace to make mistakes but that they must rise above momentary difficulties and finish every exercise with dignity and poise.

Find ways to guide each student toward one final success at the end of every lesson, if only a very modest one. For example, finish with a simple petit allegro combination followed by a port de bras that everyone can perform easily, and conclude with a révérence as in the beginning of the lesson.

Some teachers also adopt the practice of having each student step up to them after the lesson, curtsy or bow, shake hands, and thank them. This ges-

FIGURE 8

Master-teacher
Agrippina Yakovlevna
Vaganova
(1879–1951).

ture of mutual respect and appreciation provides the teacher with an opportunity to convey timely reminders, congratulate a good effort, or make a constructive criticism. It also gives the student a chance to ask brief questions about the day's lesson.

Whenever appropriate, urge students to remain in the classroom after their lesson to practice the steps or combinations they found troublesome. And encourage the better students to help those who are struggling. Such practices might require you to allow a few extra minutes between scheduled classes, extending your work day a bit or even cutting into your per-hour earnings. But such sacrifices are extremely beneficial to your students. They demonstrate a conscientiousness that, it is hoped, your students will emulate.

THE LESSON PLAN

The great Soviet master-teacher Agrippina Vaganova left us an important legacy. Her approach to teaching classical dance and the systematic method she developed in devising her syllabus of instruction have produced some of the world's greatest dance artists for over three generations.

During a televised interview Maya Plisetskaya said of Vaganova, "She was an absolute genius. Of her three thousand students, twenty-five hundred would never have become dancers were it not for Vaganova." Keep in mind that nearly *all* of her students danced professionally. How many teachers can make this claim? Throughout this book you will perceive that I support many of her theories. Along with many other teachers, I have found her ideas resoundingly effective.

The core of her methodology is what I call "patterned sequentiality." This means that she laid out her curriculum in precise groupings of long-term objectives (eight one-year segments), medium-term objectives (semesters of approximately four to five months), and short-term objectives (one-month or even one-week segments). Everything done in every lesson was thoughtfully preplanned to lead her students to a specific goal or set of goals within a specific time frame.

Beginning dance teachers studying pedagogy in the former Soviet Union must regularly hand in lesson plans that are critiqued by the master-teacher in charge of their training program. This methodology is similar to the lesson-plan system adopted by many successful teachers in public and private education systems.

One of the stark contrasts between the Vaganova method and other approaches to ballet training is that in the various republics of the former Soviet Union, students nearly always remain at the same ballet school until graduation. In addition, every student is trained exclusively in the Vaganova method. Within that system, a student might study with only three or four teachers throughout the entire eight years of training. In fact, Mme. Vaganova felt that the ideal situation would be for a student to remain with the same teacher for all the training years. Many of her first students trained with her exclusively and went on to become outstandingly great artists. Among her notable students were Natalia Kamkova, Marina Semyonova, Olga Jordan, Galina Ulanova, Natalia Dudinskaya, and Irina Kolpakova (Vaganova's last student). They were all exceptional dancers who possessed the same unmistakable qualities of technical mastery, plasticity of movement, musicality, and artistic sensitivity.

By studying with the same master-teacher throughout their training, Vaganova believed students would receive essential continuity and learn to have complete trust in their teacher, avoiding the confusion that often stems from being exposed to different theories. Naturally, this concept assumes that the teacher is well trained and comfortable with all levels of the curriculum, and is also emotionally and temperamentally suited to teach all ages of students. In practice, this is seldom a reality, as the critical student-teacher temperament match-up is often lacking in one area or another.

In addition to the variety of essential ingredients that are part of all lessons, a well-constructed lesson clearly leads students toward a predetermined goal. Each lesson, therefore, should guide the student toward a definable objective. This carefully planned, systematic approach has also been adopted by many top athletic coaches. It has been one of the primary reasons for the enormous success of the gymnastic teams of the U.S.S.R. and other Eastern Bloc countries, Cuban athletic successes in boxing and baseball, and the quick rise to prominence in track and field by the former East Germans.

Soviet ballet teachers helped train instructors in China prior to 1961.

Vaganova's methods were responsible for the amazing achievement of excellence and international recognition in a culture where no significant established history of classical dance previously existed. This was accomplished in less than a decade—an amazing feat. However, the Vaganova method, in its purest form, seems to have succeeded best in cultures that adopted some sort of authoritarian central planning system.

Most Cuban and former Eastern Bloc ballet institutions oversee the training and careers of their dancers almost literally from cradle to grave. In those cultures the young nine- and ten-year-old students must attend class daily and behave well to be allowed to remain in the dance program. Under these circumstances there is usually only one avenue (the state school) to pursue dance, and a lost opportunity to enter such an institution can never be regained. There is simply no other place to study.

Things are very different in the United States, Canada, Britain, and most of western Europe due to the extraordinary emphasis on personal freedom. Even the most knowledgeable, dedicated teachers in these countries find it difficult to apply the pure Vaganova syllabus in all its regimented specificity. It is rare for Western dance teachers to have beginning students attend class every day. We must use considerable ingenuity to meet the Vaganova syllabus goal of having young students well grounded in all the basics by the end of the first three years of study. Therefore, I advocate a slightly modified application of the Vaganova syllabus—one that I have found to be efficacious over the years. These modifications make it possible to use her syllabus outline within the strictures of the "real world" attitude toward classical dance in the West, where beginning and intermediate students rarely attend classes every day.

However, I urge teachers to make modifications only after becoming thoroughly familiar with such a uniquely comprehensive methodology and after carefully considering the needs of their students. Too much deviation and relaxation of necessary strict standards dilute the material to be studied, which extends the time needed to assimilate all the essential fundamentals.

Teachers must insist upon precisely accurate execution of basic positions, poses, and steps. In the beginning, it is best to teach each step in isolation (one at a time) before allowing students to move on to combinations. Students should be allowed to progress to more advanced levels only after they succeed in thoroughly understanding preliminary stages. The Vaganova method has proven indisputably the efficacy of this approach for over sixty years.

Every individual torso and leg movement, every pose, every position, and every port de bras (arm movement) is presented to students in a precisely systematic sequence. Every stage of development of these basics has a specific musical accompaniment suggested. And even during preliminary stages, every position, pose, and step should be taught with a separate preparation and conclusion.

Nearly all movements are first learned facing the barre with both hands on the barre, then later with one hand on the barre, and finally in the center. Nearly all exercises are first practiced to the side, and only after assimilation are they executed to the front and to the back. In the beginning, exercises may seem to be rather austere. There is little latitude for embellishment, because the students have not yet developed a repertoire of different movements and connecting steps to work with. And their minds are not sufficiently developed to cope with complexities and combinations of movements.

During the early stages, combinations of movements should be avoided. Although they may be fun for students to attempt, prematurely introduced combinations of different movements only add to a beginner's confusion, resulting in a hesitant attack and tentative attitude while attempting to stumble through them. It must be remembered that the teacher is responsible for imparting not only dance technique but also the joy of learning. This comes naturally when students sense they are improving. The teacher must use creative ingenuity to ensure that each student attains progressively higher goals, rather than entertaining students with a constant variety of new material or a learning pace that is too fast.

THE BASIC STANCE

Great care should be taken to teach every beginner the basic stance (TBS). The specific details of TBS are learned in the beginning while facing the barre. They are as follows:

> BODY WEIGHT: Should be distributed evenly over the whole foot, with approximately 60 percent over the balls of the feet and 40 percent over the heels.

FEET: In the beginning, feet are placed in a relaxed (no turnout) first position (side by side with heels together).

ANKLES: Evenly align on both the outside and inside of the leg and firmly support the shin bones above the arches of the feet.

KNEES: Although the legs must be held straight, the knee joints must not be allowed to lock at their rearward extreme. This is particularly important for students with hyperextended joints. The knee should help form and control a straight legline extending from the ankle to the pelvis.

THIGHS: All four muscle groups (inner, front, outer, and rear) are pulled up under the pelvis, as if trying to lift the body upwards.

PELVIS: With the abdominal muscles active and the muscles of the buttocks held firmly, vertically align the pelvic block beneath the lower back. Do not allow the buttocks to push or tuck under.

BUTTOCKS: Keep gluteus muscles firmly flexed.

SOLAR PLEXUS: Abdominal muscles simultaneously lift and "grip" the lower rib cage.

The above ingredients of TBS form the foundation of proper and safe turnout. They are also essential to the use of one's full lung capacity, and they aid in eliminating the problem-causing arched lower back, which in turn results in loss of stability in balances and in the more complex turning and jumping movements.

Additional essential TBS ingredients are:

HANDS: Palms down, with fingers extended and lightly resting on top of the barre, wrists and elbows relaxed.

ARMS: A comfortable arm's length from the barre, reaching straight forward, shoulder-width apart.

TORSO: Shoulders and hips held horizontal—the right shoulder directly above the right hip and the left shoulder directly above the left hip.

RIB CAGE: Lower front portion held closed by the upper abdominal muscles.

CHEST: Lifted, projecting outward and upward to allow for efficient breathing.

SHOULDERS: Held down and pulled somewhat back, so the shoulder blades are flat across the back, but not pinched together.

NECK: Straight and aligned vertically above the spine and over the center of the torso when seen from the rear.

HEAD: Pulled up on the neck, eyes looking straight forward.

The student must consciously feel that the upper body is over the top of—dominating—the lower body. TBS, sometimes called *placement,* is the foundation of ballet technique and is indispensable for attaining the highest levels of technical proficiency.

FIGURE 9   *The basic stance*

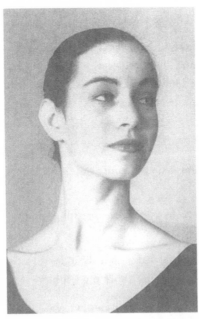 

Head turned and inclined with épaulement.   *Holding the barre with one hand.*

TURNOUT

For many years there have been conflicting opinions about the unique stresses that are placed on the body while turning out the legs. I wish to emphasize that *turnout* refers to an outward rotation of the entire leg, not just the feet. It is emphatically not a foot position. Turned out feet are merely the consequence of correctly turned out legs. This fundamental element of classical ballet is often misunderstood and consequently done incorrectly.

Turnout is the result of combining TBS with a level pelvis block, upward-lifting abdominal muscles, firm buttock muscles, and an outward rotation of the thigh muscles at the hip joint. Done properly, turnout is a graceful and elegant leg position, not a pressured pitting of flexing muscle against protesting joints. While simultaneously straightening knees, ankles, and feet, this graceful outward rotation of thigh muscles is designed to facilitate the multi-

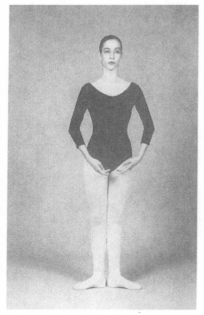

Front view with arms in the preparatory pose.

Side view with arms in third position.

FIGURE 10 *Turnout*

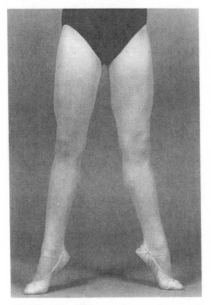

Thighs well pulled up and rotated outward.   *Knees rotated out toward the feet.*

FIGURE 11 *Turnout test*

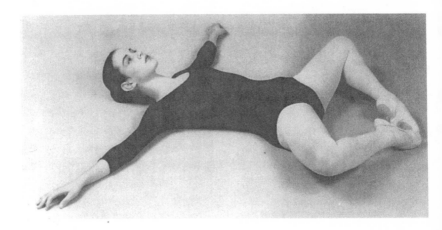

tude of ballet poses and positions and also to maintain stability and poise during sudden changes of direction while in motion. Finally, turnout helps make the many poses and positions more aesthetically pleasing.

While keeping in mind that turnout is, in theory, an absolute 180-degree rotation of one leg from the other, conscientious teachers understand that they are working with human bodies and not machines. They should carefully analyze students' turnout capabilities and instruct them on precisely how to work in a safe and constructive way.

The necessity for using turnout in classical dance stems from discoveries made by ballet theorists and teachers of the classical tradition for over two centuries. Some of these discoveries have been physiological, while most have stemmed from aesthetic and artistic concepts.

Turnout helps stabilize the torso laterally. It allows for quick, controlled changes of direction. It is one of the basic ingredients of TBS. It places the feet in the most efficient takeoff position for effective leaping. While preserving TBS, turnout also helps prevent injury when landing from certain jumps and while working on pointe.

Some artistic reasons for the use of turnout are that it presents graceful body "lines" as seen by the audience. The various poses and positions, when viewed from all sides and directions, appear clear, refined, and correct. And some unattractive views of the human body are eliminated.

Accepting turnout as a balletic necessity, then, let's discuss how to go about turning out without harming the body. First, when the body has been properly aligned according to TBS, the hips are in the position that provides the best opportunity to turn out the legs. As the thigh muscles rotate the *entire leg* outward in the hip joint, the feet maintain their straight-ahead position in relation to the legs. The result of properly turned-out thighs is turned-out feet on the floor and, most importantly, in the air while jumping or being lifted. Therefore, what appears to the uninformed viewer to be outwardly splayed feet is, in fact, the result of turning out the thigh muscles.

There are ways to check the turnout potential in students. One is to have them lie on their backs with their legs together and draw up the knees toward the chest with the feet still on the floor. Then, while keeping the feet together, let the knees separate from each other to the side, and gently press them down toward the floor *without allowing the lower back to lift off the floor.* Flexible students will be able to touch their knees to the floor in this position, while those with limited turnout will not.

When checking a student's turnout in demi-plié, make sure that the upper leg—the part between the hip and the knee—remains parallel to the line made by the foot on the floor. This alignment will hold the knee in its desired position directly above the foot all the way through to the bottom of the plié. It is essential for safe jumping.

Question: What should be done with students who lack natural turnout? Answer: The teacher needs to devise an approach that ensures that these students extend whatever turnout they have to their natural limit.

This can be done during class as follows: While holding the barre with one hand, keep the plane of the torso (alignment of the shoulders and hips) perpendicular to the barre (90 degrees); *without disturbing the above position of the torso,* turn out (rotate with the thigh muscles) the supporting leg (the leg nearest the barre) at the hip until the foot points toward the barre as close to perpendicular as possible; then, while maintaining the above position, turn

FIGURE 12   *Turnout alignment in demi-plié*

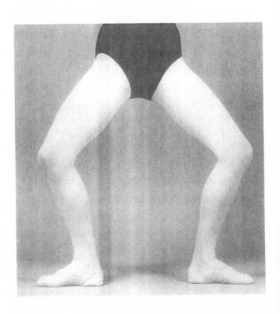

out the working leg (the leg farthest from the barre) against the strongly held supporting leg and torso. The supporting foot and ankle must not be allowed to roll inward toward the big toe. The supporting knee must not take any torquing pressure caused by the turning out of the legs. The thighs must do the work.

Students who lack natural turnout will find that their working-side leg will move forward of the torso's perpendicular plane, especially when the leg is raised sideways off the floor in second position. This is unavoidable. By working both legs during barre exercises as described above, most conscientious students can develop the strength to make some progress toward at least a minimum standard of turnout.

In the center, teachers should persist with this strict insistence upon correctly executed turnout—even with students having naturally restricted flexibility. This may mean stopping exercises occasionally to correct students and help them realign their body parts according to whatever épaulement is called for.

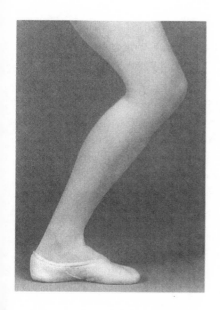
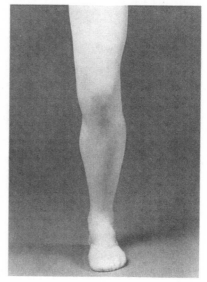

A mistake commonly made by uninformed teachers is to allow students with restricted turnout to twist the plane of their bodies, so that their working leg is perpendicular to the barre when held in second position. This makes it *appear* that they are using the working leg in the same way as other naturally turned-out students. However, this can only be accomplished by turning the plane of the torso beyond perpendicular to the barre. Students who are allowed to work this way find that they have great difficulty controlling complicated movements and balances that employ changes of épaulement. But, more importantly, students who work like this are not learning correct fundamentals that can help improve whatever turnout potential they do have.

Medical research has shown that turnout is by and large a facility given at birth. While certain strength-building aspects are required to demonstrate one's best turnout potential, every human body has built-in limitations. Students who do not possess natural turnout will be unable to significantly improve turnout through extraordinary regimens of exercise and stretching without damaging the joints. The master-teacher understands this and carefully guides students to each one's individual potential.

APLOMB

Central to TBS is the concept of *aplomb*. Mme. Vaganova used the term to refer to vertical stability and alignment. Seen from the side, the line of the dancer's body (from head to toe) will appear to incline almost imperceptibly forward, so that the shoulders are in vertical alignment over the front of the pelvis, slightly favoring the balls of the feet. The importance of perfecting aplomb and TBS cannot be overemphasized. The teacher must use whatever ingenuity and persistence are necessary to impress upon students the importance of adopting these essential fundamentals in every aspect of their dancing, including such critical moments as when leaping from the floor and while poised in flight, and also when rotating, as during pirouettes and other turning steps.

An upward-lifted vertical alignment results in maximum stability, technical consistency, and endurance. TBS and aplomb, when properly understood and employed, reduce stress and injury to joints. They also provide the

FIGURE 13

Aplomb (vertical alignment)

Notice the weight is slightly
forward, favoring the balls of the feet.

"pulled-up" attitude that results in a regal bearing, essential for the stage. And they enable dancers to safely utilize their bodies' full turnout potential.

Dancers who learn how to control TBS and aplomb also develop a strong back. They learn how to keep their rib cages closed and lifted for more efficient breathing, which is essential for endurance. The newfound poise helps contribute to an appearance of effortless accomplishment of even the most grueling combinations of movements, enabling dancers to feel as though they are defying their bodies' natural limitations, rather than lapsing into easier and more comfortable positions. And, finally, the efficient use of aplomb and TBS add considerably to dancers' longevity due to the lessening of unnecessary stress and injury.

In addition, from the viewpoint of the audience, exhilarating virtuosity, technical mastery, and a commanding stage presence are among the results seen in dancers who have mastered TBS and aplomb.

THE WELL-PLANNED BARRE

After the beginning years Mme. Vaganova discovered that a well-constructed lesson format does not require more than 30 minutes of barre work. She even demonstrated that more advanced dancers and professionals can be adequately prepared for center exercises after 20 to 25 minutes at the barre. In response to those of you who are accustomed to barres lasting up to 60 minutes, let me share how she came to this discovery.

Mme. Vaganova determined that the allegro section was the most important part of every lesson and that it should utilize at least 20 minutes of a typical 90-minute lesson. This is the minimum time in which teachers can adequately cover the entire spectrum of small jumps (petit allegro), batterie, middle jumps, and big jumps (grand allegro), all of which should be included in every intermediate and advanced lesson.

Following the barre, center exercises should be designed to prepare the student for allegro by repeating the ingredients essential to jumping and also pointe work. Although it is necessary for students to be thoroughly warmed up for allegro, it is not necessary to be *completely* warmed up at the end of the barre when the center work begins. Center exercises should be designed to complement and complete the warm-up process begun at the barre, and prepare the students for the allegro to follow. Therefore, a well-planned series of exercises in the center reduces the time needed at the barre. Remember, the barre is not an end in itself. It is only the first step toward the end (allegro).

There is often a considerable amount of time wasted during a typical lesson. First, it is advisable to teach no more than one or two new elements during each day's barre. Most barre exercises are repetitive reviews of work done during previous lessons. Variety is given through the use of different musical times (2/4, 3/4, 4/4, 6/8, etc.). Therefore, it is only the context and design of exercises that changes from day to day.

Next, many barre exercises can incorporate both half and full turns, permitting execution on both sides and reversing of combinations without stopping and restarting the music every time the dancers change sides. Valuable time may be gained by using this technique. Keep in mind that time lost anywhere during the barre and center exercises always shortens the time available for allegro at the end of the lesson.

Rather than mingling unrelated series of heterogeneous exercises, a well-planned barre interrelates exercises in a natural progression. This question will be covered more extensively later. Spend minimal time personally demonstrating exercises. Remember, the best teaching sequence is to explain exercises, demonstrating sparingly and only when absolutely necessary, then execute them without delay.

Always begin by clearly explaining to your students exactly what you want. Expect them to focus their minds sufficiently to understand every detail of your explanation. This means that teachers must develop sufficient verbal skills to be able to paint clear word-pictures. Otherwise you waste precious time by too much talking and demonstrating.

One commonly seen time-wasting approach to teaching occurs when teachers come to class without the slightest notion of what they wish to accomplish that day. They listen to the music, mentally devising each exercise, then demonstrate how they wish it to be done, or they have a student show the exercise. All this is done while the rest of the class waits. Any teacher who wastes students' valuable class time to organize exercises in such a way needs to do a better job of preplanning.

The following is an example of how Vaganova analyzed the correct method for teaching one of our most fundamental dance movements, *battement tendu with demi-plié*.

STAGE 1 (two measures of slow 4/4 time or eight measures of 3/4 time).

    a) Facing the barre in first position, slowly dégagé (extend) one leg to the side along the floor while simultaneously stretching (pointing) the foot (two counts),

    b) return the leg to first position (two counts),

    c) demi-plié (two counts),

    d) straighten the legs (two counts).

Repeat several times with the same leg. Then repeat several times with the other leg.

STAGE 2 (one measure of slow 4/4 time or four measures of 3/4 time). After practicing Stage 1 for several lessons, this phase executes each part of the exercise in a single count, but still in isolation.

    a) Dégagé the leg to the side (one count),

    b) return to first position (one count),

    c) demi-plié (one count),

    d) straighten the legs (one count).

When Stage 2 is being taught, Stage 1 is discarded.

STAGE 3 (one measure of slow 2/4 time). The opening takes place in one count and the closing enters directly into demi-plié, with the entire battement done in two counts. This means that subsequent tendus will begin with a dégagé directly from the previously done demi-plié until the exercise is concluded.

When Stage 3 is learned, Stage 2 is discarded.

STAGE 4 (slow 2/4 or 4/4 time). The complete battement tendu and demi-plié are executed in one count.

    a) Dégagé on "and" (upbeat) before the first count,

    b) close into first position directly into demi-plié on the count.

Once Stage 4 is learned, the exercise is done only in Stage 4 manner, and all previous stages are discarded. In addition, by now the students will have begun executing the exercise by holding the barre with one hand—with shoulders and hips perpendicular to the barre.

It is important to mention here that, before teaching battement tendu *with* demi-plié, Mme. Vaganova emphasized that battement tendu must first

FIGURE 14   *Battement tendu sequence (with demi-plié)*

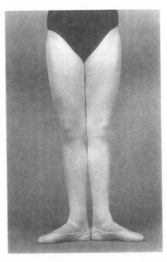

(a) First position.   (b) Dégagé side.

be taught by itself *without* demi-plié. The plié, though already familiar to the students, having been studied previously by itself in another exercise, is considered to be an added complication when combined with the simple battement tendu. Therefore, teaching battement tendu with demi-plié first would be premature—out of correct progressive sequence.

The above indicates how precisely Mme. Vaganova structured the study of a very elementary exercise. All dance movements are taught sequentially in similar manner and always with precise musical counts. After the final stage has been reached in any of the basic movements, the movement may be further enhanced by adding épaulement, small and large poses, demi-pointe where appropriate, and turns (⅛, ¼, ½, full). Even jumps are added later for some exercises, but only at the advanced level.

THE WELL-PLANNED CENTER

After approximately 30 minutes for the barre (keeping in mind that 45 minutes for beginners is appropriate), and staying mindful that we are reserving

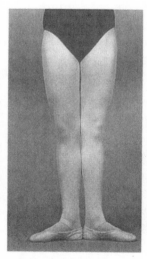
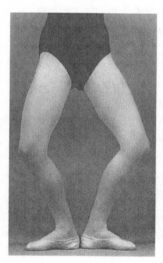
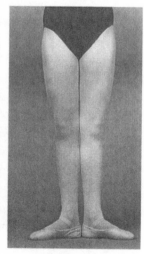

(c) Return to first position.   *(d) Demi-plié.*   *(e) Straighten the legs to original starting position.*

no less than 20 minutes for allegro, we are left, in a typical 90-minute lesson, with 40 minutes for the center work.

Just as at the barre, there are four keys to a well-organized center. The first is to alternate slow, strength-building movements, such as battement développé or battement relevé lent, with quick and light movements, such as battement frappé or petit battement sur le cou-de-pied, which focus on sudden attack and instantaneous stretching of the legs and feet. Too many sequentially slow exercises that lift and hold will indeed promote strength, but they also develop bulky musculature. Similarly, too many consecutive fast movements may develop good speed and attack but will not develop the power that is required for essentials such as sustained big poses and solid landings from big jumps.

The second key to a good center revolves around the regular use of demi-pointe. As soon as possible in the student's development, teachers should introduce demi-pointe (standing as tall as possible on the balls of the feet while raising the heels off the floor). As students progress through intermediate stages of development, work on demi-pointe should be used with increased frequency. At the advanced and preprofessional levels, demi-pointe should be used regularly at the barre and in the center.

Perfecting exercises on demi-pointe prepares the professional artist-in-the-making for the extraordinary demands of performance, because work on demi-pointe develops the level of strength in the ankles and feet that is essential for mastering the fundamentals of controlling and sustaining balance. Working on demi-pointe also raises the student's level of stamina, which is so important for the professional dancer, who is faced with demands that cause fatigue during a long day's rehearsal session, an evening's performance, or a closely spaced series of performances.

There are two arguments raised against the regular use of demi-pointe. One is that it builds large calf muscles. The other is that it causes the legs to fatigue so quickly that it spoils the artistic aspects of class work. Both arguments are based upon fallacies.

It has been demonstrated that abnormally enlarged calf muscles usually occur when demi-pointe work is done improperly—either too low or for too long a period without stretching out the muscles. Demi-pointe work, when intelligently combined with demi-pliés, usually fatigues only students who are unaccustomed to it (and who probably need it the most). The knowledgeable and observant teacher intersperses work on demi-pointe with periods of work on the whole foot, including interludes of demi-plié.

Regular use of demi-pointe obliges students to control aplomb (vertical stability), one of our essential goals, and to face the necessity of maintaining TBS and the precise placement of arms, hands, legs, and feet. The strengthening that results also accomplishes several other important goals. Female students become better prepared for work on full pointes. Male students develop better control of their landings from big jumps. And both develop better control of balance and the stamina required to perform such steps as consecutive grandes pirouettes and tours fouettés.

The third key to a productive center involves testing students' developing technical abilities by regularly calling upon them to perform exercises such as battement fondu or frappé combinations on demi-pointe. To face such tests, dedicated students must prepare their minds to arrive at every lesson ready for every challenge, while at the same time injecting performance (artistic) ingredients into each exercise.

The final key to a well-designed center is based upon what I call *the ladder of difficulty.* Some teachers who sincerely desire to develop accomplished artists often object to Mme. Vaganova's recommended high level of intensity in daily instruction. They protest, "But why give students such difficult tasks?" "Is all that preparation and demanding regimentation really necessary?" Many unenlightened teachers believe that stamina, technical command, and artistry will somehow be assimilated later after joining a company.

The answer to these questions lies in the fact that virtually no one can advance to the topmost step if allowed to linger on a ladder's lower rungs. Just as the master-teacher in music grooms students to a level of performing competence by pressing them to master their scales and to play even simple melodies and familiar tunes with finesse and beauty, master-teachers in all fields seek to guide their students beyond mere repetition. Their goal is to guide them into the highest levels of technical superiority and artistic excellence.

Most students must be shown how to meet each challenge. Teachers must develop techniques to guide students to their highest artistic capabilities. It is tragic to witness the floundering of young performers whose teachers failed to prepare them for the realities and extraordinary demands of the stage—the skills needed to perform with technical finesse and artistry. Every master-teacher develops unique ways to accomplish these goals.

It is stultifying and counterproductive for truly talented students to be kept bound to the elementary curriculum. Once students perform the rudiments of an exercise well, they should be pressed to advance to the next level of challenges. It is very important for teachers and students to realize that the rigors and the fun of dancing can bloom into exciting and stimulating artistry only when students are willing to take risks.

> *To fall seven times,*
> *to rise eight times,*
> *life starts from now*
>
> Bodhidarma

Risk-taking often means making supreme efforts, beyond the comfort zone, to perfect difficult steps or combinations. Watching talented people determinedly repeat a series of "fall-on-my-face, get-up-and-try-again" attempts, until they succeed, is a thrill to witness. It is also a great character builder for the person experiencing the challenge. On the other hand, it is sad to observe classes taught by prosaic teachers whose students go through their lessons making hesitant and timid attempts just to get through difficult passages.

Dance, at its best, should be stimulating and exciting for the audience, which can only happen when the dancer's energy is transmitted to the audience. This is achieved in the classroom by demanding teachers who insist that their students get themselves "up" before each exercise begins. Students must focus attention so they know every detail of every step to be performed. And they must be confident in their understanding of the steps, even if they are not quite able to execute each step perfectly.

Students must learn to attack the required movements with confidence and energy. They must be aggressive, while at the same time exuding artistic calm and finesse. Their movements should be large, expansive, and bold—not timid or shy. They must not be allowed to hang back or be hesitant. Naturally introverted or shy students may have difficulty with this aspect of dancing, but if they wish to succeed as professionals, they must learn this essential ingredient of theatrical artistry.

During a typical advanced lesson at the Vaganova Choreographic School in St. Petersburg (formerly Leningrad), many exercises at the barre and center are done on demi-pointe and at a very fast pace (note: "pace" not "tempo"). Quick pacing conditions the mind and nervous system to operate with a level of acuity that enables teachers and students to cover much ground in each lesson. In spite of the fast pace, every detail of every exercise is covered thoroughly.

Another beneficial side effect of this approach is that students' minds are constantly being trained to focus attention. Anyone who wanders mentally will get lost, eventually falling farther and farther behind the rest of the class.

Of course, most movements done initially in isolation can be combined later with others to provide an almost infinite variety of contexts for a given step. The Vaganova-style teaching process, when logically followed, maintains a steady progression from simplicity to complexity.

Covering the entire syllabus from Class 1 (beginners) to Class 8 (advanced) is currently an eight-year plan of daily study for children beginning at ages nine to ten in the state schools of the former Soviet republics and in other countries that employ this system. The positive results of adding intricacy to intricacy and challenge to challenge have been evident for many decades. Technical bravura and the wide-ranging classical skill of dancers trained in the Soviet Union have been witnessed and appreciated by millions of people the world over.

Teachers who understand and embrace these concepts find that their students will also readily accept and benefit from them. Once students have accepted the idea of unlimited possibilities, their minds become more receptive to every new challenge. As they do, noticeable improvement will be apparent, in spite of their normal reluctance to push beyond the comfort zone. As students see steady improvement in themselves and others, they become unquestioning believers in the idea that "I can do anything I set my mind to."

While Mme. Vaganova encouraged rapid execution, including rapid thinking and steadily increasing complexity, in the advanced levels, she emphasized slow methodicalness, mistake-free thinking, and fundamentals-focused simplicity at the elementary levels. When conducting slower-paced classes, then, the master-teacher must avoid slipping into personal boredom, which is invariably transmitted to the students, even if on a subliminal level.

One effective way to prevent boredom is for teachers to make a conscientious effort to see their classes through their students' eyes and ears. To the beginner, every tiny detail, including such things as the feel of the leotards and tights, the strange shoes, and the all-revealing mirror, is new and distracting. And for those who have had little or no previous athletic experience, demands placed upon the body often seem painfully difficult to adjust to and even a bit frightening at times.

Resist the temptation to rush the pace of awkward, fearful, or shy beginners, to skip over a student's weak or sloppy execution, or to combine exercises or steps prematurely. Show your students from the outset of their training that the highest goals and rewards in dance do not revolve around a steady diet of novel steps and combinations, but come from mastering the many details and confusing new concepts, and gaining command over their naturally reluctant bodies. They must learn that the highest achievements are attained only through hard work and discipline.

We may conclude this section with an important observation by Vera Kostovitskaya, Vaganova's former teaching assistant: "It is possible to speak of a real technique of execution only when the body, arms, and head of the dancer become the means by which the language of dance is expressed and are responsive to every emotion."

ALL-IMPORTANT ADAGIO

Clean, uncluttered dancing is the foundation of thoughtfully practiced adagio exercises. Effective adagios are comprised of slow-motion movements that are isolations of the same turns, leaps, and poses that occur during a lively and exciting allegro variation. The constructive use of adagio exercises in each lesson is of inestimable value to both performers and students, affording opportunities for the dancer to feel unfolding individual details of each movement and pose.

Throughout each aspect of daily adagio practice, TBS and aplomb are essential to correct execution and provide the stability upon which all variations are constructed. When a dance problem arises, adagio helps unravel the mystery, frees the mental clog, and releases the dancer from the bondage of unstable, inaccurate technique.

In the theater, adagio interludes provide dynamic diversity to choreography, and because these moments usually incorporate music played at slower tempos, the dancer has an opportunity to concentrate on expressive details as well as recover physically from demanding allegro dance sequences. These slower movements also give the audience an opportunity to feel the emotional range of highs and lows that good choreography and music provide.

In the beginning, adagios in class are made up of simple, connected slow movements through the use of suitable music. As time goes on, complexity is added to complexity until, at the advanced level, adagios are long, strenuous, and very challenging, even including big jumps in isolation. When designed intelligently this process has many benefits. It creates strength and increases stamina, which are vital in all aspects of dancing.

ALLEGRO: THE ESSENCE OF DANCE

Of the three fundamental elements of every lesson—barre, center, and allegro—Mme. Vaganova determined that allegro is the most important ingredient. Allegro embodies all that is uplifting about the art of dance. In her book, *Basic Principles of Classical Ballet,* she wrote, "Allegro is the foundation of the science of the dance, its intricacy and the bond of future perfection. In a burst of joy children dance and jump, but their dances and jumps are only instinctive manifestations of joy. In order to elevate these manifestations to the heights of an art, of a style, we must give it a definite form, and this process begins with the study of allegro."

When formulating the daily lesson plan, teachers should begin by determining what will be the allegro message for that day's lesson. Once this has been decided, then the barre and center are constructed to contribute to and support that end. In other words, every lesson should have an allegro theme that is divided into subthemes, or basic ingredients, related to the allegro steps to be studied. Further, it is good planning to develop a series of lessons based upon the same or similar allegro themes, so the students have an opportunity to practice new steps until they are understood and show signs of being well executed. This reinforcement process is key to instilling confidence and solid fundamentals in the students.

Edwin Denby, the well-known dance critic, observed, "The correct leap is a technical trick any ballet dancer can learn in ten or fifteen years if he or she happens to be a genius." Not everyone is a genius, but we can all learn to maximize our potential for soaring leaps.

The second law of thermodynamics states, "For every action there is an equal and opposite reaction." Applied to jumping activity, and especially to ballet allegro steps, this law can be interpreted to mean that the height and distance of the dancer's leap is determined precisely by three elements acting in concert—balance, speed, and force.

The elements of speed and force are generated by many different leg and foot muscles, including even the tiny muscles of the toes, pushing downward against the floor. In other words, the greater the amount of "action" directed downward against the immobile floor, the higher will be the "re-action" of the body elevated upward. And these two elements must also be accompanied by a stable, controlled balance.

I will attempt here to discuss a number of details, some of which may not be understood by all dance teachers. In dance, correctly executed jumps cause the dancer to appear superhuman to the observer. This means that during a jump the dancer appears to be suspended in flight, even while soaring through space.

To study this phenomenon we first need to differentiate the two basic types of jumping. The first involves leaps launched primarily from one leg alone. Examples of these are low-altitude lateral jumps (assemblé par terre, chassé, glissade), soaring leaps (grand jeté, jeté entrelacé), small traveling jumps in series (emboîté, ballonné), and big jumps in series (saut de basque and grand jeté en tournant around a circle).

The second basic type of jumping involves those that are launched primarily from both legs simultaneously, such as high-altitude semi-lateral jumps (grande sissonne ouverte), vertical jumps (changement, royale, entrechat six), and turns in the air (tours en l'air, sissonne en tournant).

Let's analyze a basic jump, *changement de pieds*, for example. Begin this jump by bending the knees, while maintaining TBS and keeping the weight evenly distributed on both feet. Then, with explosive velocity directed downward against the floor, the legs are instantly straightened, propelling the body vertically into the air. The faster the legs straighten, the higher the jump, in direct proportion.

The depth of the plié (bending of the knees prior to the jump) is also important. If a plié is shallow, the strongest of the many thigh muscles are only partly engaged. A shallow plié, even if the dancer quickly straightens the legs, does not allow the powerful thigh muscles to travel far enough to push the dancer's body more than a short distance off the floor. Such jumps appear weak and effete, even though the foot and calf muscles may have responded to the best of their ability.

Beginning dancers must be taught that such superficial efforts are unacceptable. Audiences, dance competition judges, company directors, and critics downgrade dancers who jump weakly and are passive in their attack of allegro steps. Weak jumps have an effect exactly opposite to that which audiences expect to see onstage. Weak jumps make the dancer appear smaller-than-life and severely detract from the energy and excitement of a performance. The light, soaring quality of the leap is lost, and the dancer appears earthbound and heavy. Those who dance this way either do not understand the dynamics required for jumping, or they have not sufficiently developed their leg muscles to make the required effort effective.

A powerful jump requires a deep demi-plié (knee bend); an explosive push from the floor, beginning with the thigh muscles; a complete straightening of the knee joint; and a finishing thrust (in rapid succession) with the calf muscles, the ankle, the foot, and the toes. This is a top-down concept, meaning that a strong jump should always begin from the upper leg and work down through the toes.

Teachers also understand that there are several small jumps that do not require a big effort to execute properly. Many petit allegro steps may be done with a minimum of upper leg thrust and are designed to attract attention to the quickness of the feet.

When jumps are complicated by the use of preparatory movements, balance and weight distribution become critical. Following whatever preparatory step is given prior to the jump, it is imperative that the dancer be balanced over the supporting foot, at the moment of taking off into the air. And finally, the arms often participate in helping the dancer take off into the jump.

All these ingredients must be coordinated perfectly to achieve the maximum result without showing apparent effort and without disturbing TBS and vertical stability. It requires hard work and discipline to assimilate these ideas and develop a jumping technique that thrills and excites an audience.

Some Head Specifics

The head must be aligned directly above the thrusting leg(s) when executing vertical jumps. The dancer exerts leg-muscle force downward against the floor directly under the head while simultaneously pulling the head upwards with the neck muscles.

When performing lateral jumps, the head is inclined slightly in the direction of the intended movement. However, the neck muscles still pull the head strongly up into the air, without showing any strain, of course.

Some Arm Specifics

Most jumps use the arms in specific ways. Upper and lower arms, wrists, and hands must be coordinated with the leap's accompanying leg movements. If used incorrectly, they could cancel out the thrusting action of the legs. These arm movements (port de bras), taught together with the jumping action of the legs and feet, also provide a coordinated elevation of the body. For example, many big jumps begin by quickly raising one of the legs to start the leap. This working leg movement is nearly always accompanied by an explosive jump from the other, supporting leg out of a deep demi-plié. The role of the arms is to provide a coordinated port de bras in conjunction with the effort of the legs. All of these movements, together with good balance, are necessary to achieve maximum results.

Some Thigh Specifics

Because of the emerging science of sports medicine in recent years, we have learned that every muscle is composed of three different types of muscle fibres: quick-twitch, medium-twitch, and slow-twitch. In addition, we have the concept of core fibers from ancient Oriental physiology. Most athletic programs prior to 1960 were concerned with only one type of fiber at a time. Since the early 1960s, a small but ever-growing number of pioneers in physiology began developing programs that affected two (and on rare occasions three) types of fibers at a time. The result has been a steady breaking of world's records in many athletic events, and a general improvement in the skills of athletes (and dancers). High school and college girls have bettered many men's Olympic Games records posted prior to the 1940s.

The only area largely unexplored by Western sports medicine is the mysterious "core fiber" reportedly known to Oriental martial arts masters and Tibetan monks. This fiber is rumored to enable a person to virtually defy gravity with the height and distance of leaps and with amazing feats of strength and endurance.

I was able to obtain the following details on how to develop core fiber jumping technique from an elderly Japanese martial arts master. His instructions were, "While bending the knees, which are kept directly above the balls of the feet . . . simultaneously expel all 'limitness' out of the body, including 'old airs' from the lungs and all 'grounding thoughts' from the mind." He explained that some of these grounding thoughts are limitations, preconceptions, suppositions, preferences, and biases. He went on to say, "When all of the 'old airs' are out of the lungs and all 'grounding thoughts' out of the mind, *become the air!*" By this he meant that while inclining your head upward and looking into the sky, you throw your hands upwards and catapult yourself vertically with an explosive burst of energy, while becoming as light as the air.

Although the above may seem merely curious or just mildly interesting to some readers, there is some food for thought for serious dance artists. In the above discussion it can be seen that training the mind becomes one of the main ingredients in developing core fiber.

In recent years psychology has begun to play an important role in the development of athletes. "Imaging" is a relatively new concept but has been widely accepted in helping to create superstar athletes.

Before every shot, the great golfer Jack Nicklaus stands behind his ball "seeing" in his mind the precise flight of the ball and exactly where it will land. High jumper Dwight Stones, a former world-record holder, would stand at the end of the runway "seeing" in his mind each step of his run to the bar followed by a mental picture of himself soaring over the bar. He would repeat this "imaging" several times until he felt imbued with sufficient confidence to attempt his jump. Top athletes in many sports can be seen "imaging" before their effort. Watch for signs of this as you view sporting events.

To those unfamiliar with the term *imaging*, the meaning may be simplified by explaining that individuals focus thought so keenly that they "see" themselves in their minds precisely achieving their goals. Could these ideas help to train classical ballet dancers?

Some Foot Specifics

With most outstanding jumpers, such as the legendary Vaslav Nijinsky, foot shape and foot positions while leaping were similar to those of a bird. When Nijinsky flexed his foot upwards at the ankle, the distance between the tip of the heel and the ankle bone was almost exactly the same as between the heel and the toes. In Nijinsky's case, these measurements between ankle bone, heel, and toes were accompanied by a disproportionately sized Achilles tendon.

Studies of Dinka and Watusi tribesmen in Africa, known for their exceptional leaping prowess, have shown that Achilles tendon size, flexibility, and length help determine how high a human can leap. Analogized to lower animals and leaping insects, the rear legs of the frog, the flea, and the grasshopper are almost totally Achilles-type tendons and muscles.

In dance, an artistically executed jump incorporates all of the aforementioned dynamic ingredients together with an undisturbed basic stance. Naturally, modifications of balance and weight distribution are introduced to conform with the emotional content and choreographic design. In addition, jumps must be "frozen" for an instant at the leap's apex, so that the dancer appears suspended in midair. In other words, dancers should arrest their pose in flight, so it can be more clearly seen by the viewer.

Some Breathing Specifics

A brief mention of breath control while jumping is in order. In most cases it is best to inhale at the moment of muscular exertion. Therefore, as dancers are preparing for their leap they are also preparing to inhale. This moment might be as simple as inhaling while doing a relevé prior to a vertical jump from two legs, or it might be during a preparatory glissade or chassé that precedes a big lateral jump off one leg.

Dancers must not get in the habit of holding their breath during a series of jumps. They must learn to exhale during logical interludes between jumps, so that they are ready to inhale again when it is time for their next big effort. However, this does not mean that they must breathe between every jump.

It is also important for dancers to guard against relaxing their bodies involuntarily as they exhale, usually when landing from big jumps or other extraordinary efforts. Inexperienced students often have difficulty with this concept. Not controlling this important detail of breathing easily results in a collapse of TBS and aplomb.

Stamina

During the final minutes of every lesson, the teacher should devise a series of vigorous jumps that force the muscles to surpass their former limits. These should be done sequentially with no pause to rest. This is the moment for the teacher to urge the students to extend themselves and surpass previous efforts. Typical commands for the teacher to give at this time might be:

"You are in control of your body? *Take charge!*"

"Tell your body what it *must* do! Don't let it tell you what it wants to do!"

"Take off and fly!"

"*I can't* is just a negative idea. Don't let an idea control you!"

If done in the right context, students will end the lesson with muscles momentarily exhausted, in a state of "rubberiness," but their spirits will be singing with enthusiasm. This is one of the training secrets that prepares the human mind to give peak performances during an exhausting solo, or to continue working at peak day after day during even the most demanding touring schedule.

As soon as their teacher is certain they understand, students should cultivate the above jumping dynamics. Occasionally, dancers or athletes such as basketball star Michael Jordan will have an extraordinary instinct about jumping. They usually have no idea why or how they are able to jump so high. Such individuals, referred to as *natural jumpers,* are a joy to behold. It gives the viewer a thrill to watch such soaring leaps. Teachers need to find ways to get their "ground-huggers" and "lead-legs" up into the air, so they can also experience the thrill.

WEIGHT

In dance, this term does not refer to how much a dancer weighs. Weight is a basic concept that refers to the solid or stable feeling one has while standing on or moving across the floor.

Earlier in this chapter we discussed TBS. TBS gives the dancer a lifted, weightless feeling, even while at the bottom of a grand plié (deep knee bend). This lifted feeling should be maintained during all dance movements, especially during jumps. Here we uncover a seeming paradox—the dancer must simultaneously experience solid *weightiness* and airy *weightlessness*. Let's take a moment to consider this concept and try to see how it works.

The dancer's mind must differentiate between upliftedness and positive solid contact with the floor. This idea is analogous to the concepts of jumping previously discussed, where one must increase dynamic pressure in the lower half of the body while bending the knees into a plié before leaping. This pressing down, or squeezing against the floor, is like compressing a coiled spring or drawing a bow string before releasing an arrow.

While dancing, positive contact with the floor is derived partly from keeping body weight constant through balanced and controlled TBS. Although the dancer's body weight is aligned over the entire foot, we have already explained that it should always slightly favor the balls of the feet rather than the heels (an approximate 60/40 percent split is recommended). As the dancer moves, this weight distribution must remain constant regardless of how complex the movement. This helps the dancer feel always in balance, facilitating precise control, especially while shifting balance from one leg to the other and during quick changes of direction.

Another important aspect of the weight concept has to do with the dancer's eyes. Dancers remain so solidly focused on the meaning of every gesture involving the head and arms that they draw the audience up onto the stage to experience the drama along with them. The depth and breadth of the character being portrayed is expressed through the dancer's eyes, so that every movement conveys an aura of authenticity and authority and a solid believability. It is this special type of "weightiness" that Maya Plisetskaya possessed when she gave us the wonderful legacy of her *Dying Swan*, that revealed the torment of Yuri Vladimirov's tragically insane *Ivan the Terrible*, that helped

Alicia Alonso share her definitive *Giselle,* and that caused Nora Kaye to almost literally become Hagar in Antony Tudor's *Pillar of Fire.*

FREEZE-FRAME PRECISION

Although dancing is fundamentally rhythmic, organized movement, it is also
based upon a sequential series of poses performed smoothly one after another. Dancing can be analogized to the illusion that is created by a motion
picture or by an animated cartoon. Although the movie or cartoon provides
the appearance of continuous movement, it is actually comprised of a series
of individual snapshots, or frames, running smoothly in sequence through
the projector.

An example of these sequential movements, a one-minute grand allegro
variation (solo) that is performed as a continuous flow of movements (jumps,
turns, and beats connected by specially designed linking steps) is actually
comprised of dozens of individual poses performed one after another in rapid
succession. Even while leaping through the air, the accomplished dancer
effectively "freezes" all foot, leg, arm, head, and body movements for a moment in whatever pose is given for that particular leap. This is done so that
the body appears suspended or arrested in flight. The required pose is struck
at the apex of the leap and is then held as long as possible during the rest of
the jump until the landing. Likewise with the various types of turning and
beating steps. Each type of turn, and each series of beats, must be done incorporating a specific body position that the audience should be able to see
clearly defined.

Another example of this idea can be seen during the study of jumping
steps that incorporate a beat in the air. These include all entrechats, battus,
and cabrioles. The precise moment when the body is most tranquil during
most jumps is at the apex. When dancers initiate a jump there is a burst of
energy as they leave the floor while ascending to the top of the jump. The legs
are thrusting. The arms are being raised toward the required pose. The whole
body is energized.

When dancers reach the apex of the jump there is a very brief "quiet"
moment just before they begin their descent back to the floor. At this moment the beat should take place and the required pose should be established,

because they are momentarily "at rest" in midair. The audience's eye can arrest the movement, allowing its image to be established in memory.

If a teacher allows students to practice such movements without this sense of integrity, known commonly in the dance world as *line,* they will develop an inability to execute consistently clean movements—a situation that the practiced eye can see all too often, even among professional dancers. This inconsistency causes audiences to feel that some dancers are continually struggling to adjust their body parts during the leap or throughout the pose, movement, or variation. These dancers transmit a feeling that they are not in complete control.

Dancers who do not learn these principles appear to the audience to be dancing "through" each given pose, rather than executing their steps cleanly "in" the required pose. This fuzziness, or vagueness, often leaves the perceptive viewer somewhat uneasy and worried about whether or not the dancer will be able to get through the routine without a faux pas. TBS, aplomb and line are extremely important concepts of dancing that must be understood and perfected. All master-teachers understand their importance and work diligently to impart this knowledge to their students.

ELBOW ROOM

Master-teachers avoid crowding too many students into their classrooms. It is true that studio owners have many expenses. Rent has a way of increasing steadily, utility bills continue to creep upwards, and local newspapers raise their advertising rates. One solution is to enlarge the size of the class. However, it is not possible to do justice to all your students with more than twenty or so in class. And fewer is better for beginners where individual scrutiny is essential.

No master-teacher, however capable and perceptive, working in a crowded class, can provide the optimal level of scrutiny and personalized supervision of so many feet, knees, arms, and personalities. And no teacher can properly guide so many minds, each of which is unique and requires personalized attention. When well-prepared teachers divide a class of twenty students into lines during the center and allegro exercises, they are able to monitor each student, because each one can be kept within view at all times.

At the barre, ensure that each student has adequate barre space, and enough extra for you to intervene when correction is necessary. It is not uncommon to find overcrowded class situations where students are obliged to hang onto the piano or backs of chairs. Or they have to stand so close together that nearly every exercise must be done facing diagonally toward or away from the barre. Such situations are unacceptable to a master-teacher. Students must be able to work at the barre so that their legs can be fully extended forward and backward, without their needing to turn away from the barre to avoid colliding with their neighbors.

Adequate spacing has greater import than mere comfort or convenience. It also pertains directly to two important stage concepts that must be learned—maintaining the proper interval between dancers and keeping in line.

In time, students who are crowded at the barre or in the center tend to curtail the full extension of their limbs and the broadness of their movements. If habitually repeated during their formative years of training, students may develop a mind-set that inhibits strong, assertive attack. This problem is readily observed among students who move their arms and legs hesitantly. It can also be a serious problem with professional dancers who do not learn the importance of boldly expanding their movements and poses. Such disabilities are the result of training with teachers who allow their students to shrink their movements rather than learn to expand and enlarge them—a problem due to overcrowding.

Because expansive movements and gestures are essential theatrical qualities, an inhibited way of working is utterly inimical to the stage. Teachers who think only about squeezing more bodies into a classroom are drilling into their students' minds and bodies patterns of movement that are absolutely wrong for the stage.

When moving the students from barre to center, the teacher should divide the class into small groups. Tell each student exactly where to stand in relation to the other students in the group. If it is necessary to group the students into more than one line, you should position the back line so you can see each student clearly when looking between the front-row students.

It is important that you take sufficient time to position students, since you should attempt to see everything that goes on during every exercise and correct the slightest mistake. If you try to work with more than two or three lines of students at a time, you will probably be unable to see, let alone correct, many of your students' mistakes. This is a serious disservice to those in your charge.

Working with overcrowded classes also prevents you from maintaining the requisite level of precision. Overcrowding also causes center work and adagio work to proceed at an overly slow pace, causing students to become bored and lose the necessary edge of mental alertness and precision. In addition, students' muscles begin to cool down after the barre, which could result in injuries when the energetic "attack" movements and allegro steps begin. Attention to such details is a sign of a well-organized, thoughtful teacher.

FIGURE 15   *Center exercise spacing diagram*

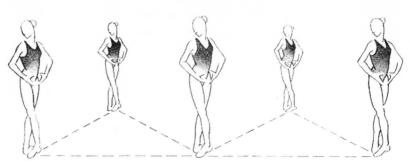

Dancers are placed evenly in contiguous equidistant triangles.

TO ERR IS HUMAN

Most students must be trained to attack their movements. They must not hold back out of a fear of making mistakes. This prideful reluctance must be eradicated. The master-teacher does not let ego get in the way of the pursuit of excellence.

The master-teacher creates an ambience that says, "It's OK to make mistakes—even inevitable—but we can learn from them." The master-teacher finds ingenious ways for every student to succeed at perfecting all aspects of their poses, steps, or combinations. I find it useful in my own teaching to remind the class that there are bound to be mistakes when one strives for perfection. When a mistake happens while a student is making a supreme effort, such a mistake is bound to be a *big* one, and both student and teacher will see more clearly what needs improvement.

Students must also be taught to maintain composure in the face of adversity, which includes recovering immediately and gracefully after momentary slips or concentration lapses during class. They must even learn to remain composed after falls to the floor that might occur from time to time in class (or onstage for that matter). This controlled composure is a sign of true professionalism.

Never allow students to begin their movements with a tentative, weak attack. This may happen when experienced students lose concentration and do not learn an exercise. They may hang back and wait to see what their neighbors are doing. Nervous eyes are a giveaway. Also, beginners inevitably inhibit their movements for fear of making mistakes and being ridiculed by their peers. Prepare for it. Help your students realize that everything that takes place in the classroom revolves around struggling with the bombardment of new information. And *come down like thunder* on anyone who ridicules someone else's unsuccessful effort.

As a brief aside: it is amazing how many spectacular innovations, not only in dance but also in gymnastics, ice-skating, and other similar activities, began as mistakes that were seen by the perceptive master-teacher and choreographer as potential enhancements to an otherwise prosaic movement or combination.

MUSIC IN CLASS

Do not fall prey to teaching by rote; for example, be wary of becoming a waltz-time addict. Many teachers tend to associate certain steps, exercises, and combinations with a limited selection of musical tempos and rhythms. Even if you love the waltz and associate dancing with it, do not allow 3/4 time to dominate your classes. The vast repertoire of music written in 6/8, 2/4, 4/4, and so forth offers opportunities to enrich every lesson with a variety of interesting music. In its full range, music is the dancer's stock in trade. Your students will receive an invaluable education if you expose them to the full panorama of the language of music.

Mme. Vaganova long ago discovered that many exercises commonly done in 3/4 time are more accurately taught and executed in 4/4 or 2/4 time. Ronds de jambe par terre and en l'air are two such examples. Yet how many of us consistently (or even exclusively) use a waltz for these exercises? I do not mean to say that ronds de jambe should never be done in 3/4 time. In fact, intermediate and advanced students should be astute enough musically to perform exercises with a variety of accompaniment.

Ronds de jambe par terre are correctly performed with steady, even movements during each segment—around and through. It is improper to do a strong and quick passé par terre to catch the strong 3/4 time downbeat (count 1), and then do a softer and smoother circular rotation during the weaker beats (counts 2 and 3). Executing this exercise in 4/4 or 2/4 time helps to achieve this aim, as the accents are more regular and evenly spaced. In addition, it is easier to work within the music when using 2/4 or 4/4 time. By this I mean that the exercise can be easily performed at half tempo or double tempo with these rhythms. It can be readily seen that this is not so easily done with music in 3/4 time.

In contrast, grands battements jetés can be done very nicely with a strong waltz tempo, closing firmly on the downbeat (count 1) and beginning the dégagé on count 3. Using different musical selections to provide variety for each step helps students develop an ear for music's nuances, and frees them from the sweatshop mentality that treats music as nothing more than rhythmic background for getting through exercises.

Nikolai Tarasov, a former outstanding Soviet teacher and author on pedagogy, said, "To interrupt the inner link with the musical theme is to depart from interpretive movement into mere technique. The musical theme must always manifest itself as the pupil's artistic, emotional, conscious feeling for dance, as a vital, fully conscious choreographic cantilena." In other words, true artists dance the music, not just to the music. They almost literally "become" the music.

Teachers who use recorded music should search out records that have long bands of thirty-two to sixty-four measures of the same steady tempo. It is also desirable to select records that have a four-measure musical introduction rather then the standard two chords. The four-measure musical introduction establishes the tempo and character of the music, and makes it easier for students to attack the exercise from the beginning.

If used cleverly, records can provide a variety of interesting musical selections. It is not necessary to be a slave to the exercise indicators on the album jacket. For example, music indicated for grands pliés can easily be adapted for nearly any adagio-type exercise, and music indicated for battements frappés is often perfect for petit allegro combinations. Whenever I teach with records, I use two long-playing albums, mixing selections from one to the other, so that the music properly reflects the character of the exercise while providing a wider variety of selections. In addition, if records are being used over a period of time for the same class, they should be alternated regularly with other albums, so that the students do not get overly familiar with the music. Nothing is more boring than to hear the same music day after day. This applies to live piano accompaniment as well.

To provide the most flexible use of records, it is essential to have access to a variable-speed turntable. See chapter 6 for a more detailed discussion of sound systems.

I do not recommend using tapes. Teachers who use them are restricted by the order of musical selections that are recorded on the tape. It is awkward to search for different bands on a tape deck and nearly impossible to mix bands on different sides of tapes. This is so even if you make up your own tapes.

I believe that we will eventually see instructional music published on compact disks. The design of CD players makes it possible to skip from one band to another and one disk to another easily, and the sound quality is far superior to records and tapes. However, there is not a great deal of incentive to use this technology at the present time, because those who make and sell records profit from continuing follow-up sales of records as they wear out. Due to their durability, CDs last much longer, cutting down on potential profits.

If you work with a live accompanist, insist on the four-measure introduction. Also, choose an accompanist who is willing to expand his or her repertoire beyond preprinted anthologies of typical ballet classroom music comprised of familiar tunes that add little to your students' musical education. Also, discourage repetitive use of familiar melodies from ballets such as *Swan Lake, The Nutcracker,* or *Coppelia.* Instead, ask your accompanist to create a varied and interesting repertoire. A good accompanist should also learn to interpolate music that may not originally have been written for dance. Encourage experimentation with improvisation and appropriate original composition.

Readers might be interested to know that most of the music played for ballet classes in the state academies of the former Soviet Union is either improvised or variations on themes from the classical repertoire. In my judgment, it is not a good idea to inject pop music into the classical dance lesson. These tunes might provide some fun for the lesson, but the character of this style of music is usually not conducive to expanding awareness of the art of classical dance during the formative years.

The master-teacher monitors the accompanist since the dance lesson provides most students with their basic musical education. In addition to rhythm and tempo, the mood or spirit of each exercise must be considered. Scrupulous attention to these details will greatly enrich the atmosphere of the lesson.

VARIETY

Variety in lesson planning also depends on how exercises are designed. Well-designed exercises can be done not only from the right and the left sides but they can also be reversed. If your students know that you will regularly call upon them to reverse exercises, they will develop the mental facility of visualizing what they must do, rather than executing repetitions by rote. Through the process of mental imagery, students learn to comprehend the fundamentals of movement, the overall *shape* of a combination, and eventually the principles of dance itself.

The ability to visualize the shape of exercises is a particularly valuable asset for professional dancers. Professionals must learn how to adapt quickly to choreographic alterations and last-minute changes. It is commonplace for dancers to be called upon to fill in for colleagues who are injured or ill. Dancers who have trained their minds to be adaptable are valuable assets to a company and will find themselves in demand by ballet masters and choreographers.

CHAPTER 9

Related Dance Forms

When the music and dance create with
accord . . . their magic captivates both
the heart and the mind.

Jean Georges Noverre

The advent of the television satellite has created an increased interest in all
performing arts. Providing instant access, this form of communication per-
mits audiences all over the world to watch live performances of the great artists of our day. And, of course, videotaping gives us a permanent record of
past performances to view over and over. This instant exposure to larger audiences seems to encourage artistic luminaries in one field to cross over into
other areas—dancers trying to act, singers trying to dance, and actors trying
to sing. Small wonder that some teachers feel pressured to liberalize their curriculum and offer a smorgasbord of diverse forms.

This observation prompts the question "Should a variety of dance styles
be taught to younger students?" We have determined that dance, in the
broadest sense, is organized movement normally accompanied by music. It
encompasses all possible uses of the human body to convey feelings, emotions, or ideas, which I call the Dancerly Paradigm:

Through a purposeful (or serendipitous) combination of movements,
poses, gestures, music, costumes, and background settings . . . various
emotions, feelings, and ideas are conveyed from one person to another.

Within the paradigm are innumerable dance styles. Historically, most developing civilizations have experienced several categories of dance forms, including sacred dance, social dance, seduction dance, story-telling dance, and combat dance.

In some cultures, these different styles were kept rigidly separated, and sometimes harsh punishments were inflicted on those who dared intermix them. In other instances they were prohibited entirely. Depending on the mores of the culture, some of those categories have been referred to as the classical dance of that particular culture or that era.

Throughout history the division of these dance forms has become increasingly blurred. Today, there seems to be less agreement on what is considered classical dance. Even the term *classical ballet* is given different definitions by authorities in the field, so that one finds a great variety of so-called classical ballet styles taught in U.S. ballet schools.

For the sake of clarity, when I use the terms *ballet* and *classical dance,* I refer specifically to the dance style that was handed down from Jean Georges Noverre through Carlo Blasis to Enricco Cecchetti (Italian school) and from Noverre through Johansson and August Bournonville to Pavel Gerdt and the Legat brothers (French school). Also the terms *ballet* and *classical dance* refer to the carefully studied analysis by Vaganova of both methods, which evolved into a modern system incorporating the best ingredients of both.

Since the mid-1960s, a standard for classical dance has been adopted by the organizing committees and judges for international ballet competitions held throughout the world, most notably in Varna, Bulgaria; Moscow, Russia; Japan; Jackson, Mississippi; and Lausanne, Switzerland among others.

The standard recognized by all schools and international judges and critics emphasizes the qualities that epitomize the ideal classical dancer, who would be at home dancing *Swan Lake, Giselle,* or *Sleeping Beauty* as well as ballets by contemporary choreographers. Using these criteria, I have found it of little benefit to beginning or intermediate students who aspire to a career in a classical ballet company to mix other dance styles simultaneously with their study of classical ballet.

Every dance style, which I differentiate from popular dance fads, has a unique theoretical base with its own unique pattern of movements. These patterns and theories often stand in stark contrast from one style to another. Advanced students and professional dancers may benefit by exploring these sometimes conflicting ideas. However, beginning and lower-intermediate students are usually confused by such exploration and derive little artistic benefit from it.

Students who wish to become professional ballet dancers are well advised to concentrate, during the first five or six years of study, on the classical curriculum until the fundamentals have become solidly fixed within the muscle memory of the nervous system. As we have already established, it usually takes eight or nine years of serious study for talented beginners to become skilled professionals. Other dance styles such as jazz, modern, and tap (which may later contribute to helping students become more valuable company members) can be introduced when students reach more advanced levels of technical proficiency. Prematurely introducing other styles confuses the students and distracts them from their primary goal, which is to establish a foundation of solid, secure ballet technique.

Other dance styles, though legitimate themselves, serve as enrichment for the mature ballet dancer, but cannot help primary students achieve their goals. Introducing other styles during the final two or three years of ballet training achieves the desired result. Just as this careful separation of dance styles is applied to classical dance training, the concept is equally applicable to the tap student, the modern dance student, or the jazz student.

It is interesting to note that if a student decides to change to another primary dance style after studying ballet conscientiously for four or five years, the ballet background noticeably accelerates the learning process of the new style. This makes it possible for the ballet trained dancer to attain the advanced level of the new style in a much shorter time than would normally be required.

Conversely, students who begin their dance training with modern, tap, ballroom, folk, or jazz usually find it quite difficult to adjust to the discipline of the classical ballet curriculum. They usually require several years of classical dance education before beginning a career in ballet. I hasten to add that, while these observations are generally true, there have been exceptions.

PARTNERING

Partnering is an essential aspect of classical dance with which every career-track ballet student should be thoroughly familiar. The technique should be taught only after girls have become strong on pointe and boys are physically able to handle and lift relatively heavy weights. Teaching partnering prematurely requires male partners to be constantly on guard to save the girls from disaster—from falling, collapsing, or losing balance and control. Girls who are weak on pointe, and males who do not know how to handle heavy weights, can also experience serious injuries, particularly when attempting lifts. Partners must learn to work as a well-blended team and to trust each other.

Before beginning the study of partnering techniques, the girls must have already developed a thorough understanding of alignment and TBS. They must understand the importance of maintaining their alignment within each pose or step *even when they feel off center or off balance!* If they constantly try to correct their balance while being held or lifted by a partner, it becomes virtually impossible for the male to find the correct alignment for the required pose or position.

The requirement to hold oneself together must be adhered to during all poses, turns, and lifts. The key to attaining this goal is mutual trust. Boys must be able to inspire a feeling of complete confidence within their female counterparts. In turn, girls need to know that their partner will always be there to help whenever a need arises.

The girls must work on feeling light and lifted up at all times while being partnered. Each time a lift or a balance is called for they must fearlessly attack the required pose or transitional movement, confident that their partner will provide whatever support is needed. Nothing stultifies artistic imagery more than a male partner attempting to lift a flaccid ballerina who jumps weakly into her lifts or makes superficial attempts to strike her poses.

Another aspect of good partnering that dancers often ignore is the importance of eye contact with each other during appropriate choreographic moments. It is blatantly unartistic for partners to play to the audience while ignoring their relationship with one another.

The male partner has two main functions. He must provide a romantic interest for his partner—the essence of the classical pas de deux (duet)—and he must add special emphasis to his partner's elegance and refinement. He helps her turn more, leap higher, and sustain her extensions and poses beyond her normal capabilities.

A harmoniously unified duo creates an illusion of superhuman ability. Many traditional ballet roles portray mythical personages, spiritual beings, or transcendental ideas. Also, in the repertoire of contemporary choreography, partnerships often extend beyond the traditional pas de deux to threesomes (pas de trois), foursomes (pas de quatre), and so forth, which provide virtually limitless choreographic design possibilities.

A good male partner develops special sensitivities regarding line and composition. He learns to sense how his poses complement his partner's. He understands balance and alignment, so his partner need not struggle to feel her own center and correct position. He also learns how to use his legs as the foundation for lifting. He is always attentive to the physical and emotional needs of his partner. He learns to distinguish between firm support and holding tightly, and he provides the ideal masculine romantic counterpart when appropriate.

Since trust is the cornerstone of good partnering, it is worth noting that many male dancers have made successful careers as partners without being outstanding solo dancers themselves. Ballerinas are always looking for solid, attentive partners.

Onstage, the epitome of classical ballet is the romantic pas de deux. This dance relationship emphasizes the difference between male and female roles. It is appropriate here to mention some important aspects of these roles and how master-teachers deal with the differences.

It should be part of students' training to learn how to dress and groom themselves appropriately for class, so that the girls appear clearly feminine, and the boys appear clearly masculine. Older girls, for example, might use a little makeup or wear close-fitting earrings during class. They should always have their hair neatly combed and fastened, so that it does not interfere with the various movements. Using some flowers or ribbon in the hair in good taste adds a nice touch and also gives them a sense of individuality. They might also wear either plain or colorful skirts that complement their leotards. The girls should appear gracious, attractive, and modest.

On the other hand, prettiness and effeminate behavior in male students are out of place. This includes wearing attire commonly associated with women, even if it is in vogue (for example, flamboyantly designed leotards, earrings, long hair). Such habits are not indicative of the art of classical dance and are in poor taste when exhibited inappropriately onstage or in the class-room. This applies to heterosexual males as well as those who may be inclined toward homosexuality. The art of classical dance in no way benefits from flaunting one's sexual predilection.

Qualities such as strength, protectiveness, courtesy, and courage are integral to many male roles in the classical repertoire and are essential to provide the masculine contrast with their female partners. Effeminate behavior patterns incorporated into basic habits such as standing, walking, gesturing, and speech should be discouraged.

In the theater, the classical romantic libretto is often included in a company's repertoire, even in contemporary choreography. Young male students should be encouraged to overcome their normal athletic exuberance and taught how to perform gracefully without slipping into mannered femininity. The best way for teachers to impart such matters to young impressionable students is to be role models. Remember, your manner and personality are frequently your students' copybook. Students usually emulate teachers they admire. If you are respected and admired by your students, your actions will have a strong influence on them.

CHARACTER DANCE

In the context of classical ballet, character or ethnic dance seems to be a dying art form. Sadly, it has become an increasingly neglected aspect of the training required of classical ballet dancers. This neglect stems from the fact that we have gone through the transition of supporting a handful of large companies that in the past emphasized the classical repertoire to the present condition of having many companies that are too small to stage full-length classics. Most of these small twelve- to twenty-dancer companies have contemporary, eclectic repertoires that do not require expertise in character dance. This is regrettable because training in these special dance styles helps dancers experience the colorful flair and feeling of freedom that are associated with character dance.

As the need for expertise in character dance disappears, the demand for well-trained teachers in this medium also diminishes. Well-taught folk dances contribute to a student's understanding of the flavor and character of different world cultures. Unfortunately, the new generation of choreographers has little knowledge of ethnic dance styles, nor are they much interested in using them in their creations.

The term *character dance* refers not only to special steps and movements that are unique to particular countries or regions but also deals with the subtleties of social interactions. In some instances these dances form the foundations of religious conviction. Therefore, when teaching these styles of dance, far more than superficial romantic male-female relationships should be introduced. Students fortunate enough to be given the opportunity to learn these styles benefit professionally and artistically from the experience.

In spite of the loss of emphasis on character dance, there still remain in the repertoire of many classical companies ballets such as *Swan Lake, Coppelia, Giselle,* and *Sleeping Beauty.* These ballets require expertise in such folk mediums as polonaise, mazurka, czardas, Spanish, and tarantella. Companies that neglect the subtleties of training in these unique styles produce weak and unsatisfying performances, despite excellent dancing by artists in the other classical roles.

Years ago, before the age of neoclassicism and modern ballet, many ballets in the repertoire required dancers to perform a variety of dance styles. Dancers had to learn the special characteristics and peculiarities of these dances, often from specialists in the field. These dances, which were later woven into the story lines of the ballets being staged, helped provide a more authentic atmosphere for the ballet as a whole.

In contrast, much of today's choreographic emphasis is based upon abstract images that arise in the minds of choreographers when they listen to a chosen musical composition or develop a theme. Most present-day choreographers tend to avoid tradition and plunge into their own psyches for composition ideas.

Despite this trend, there still exist a few companies that perform the classics. They require competence in the character-dance mediums, and corps members are expected to perform them with the same élan as their classical roles.

My experience and study in the matter lead me to conclude that teachers should offer at least the basics of character dance in their curriculum. If you are a teacher who has not, yourself, learned character dance, hire a professional to visit now and then as a guest teacher. Not only are these dances colorful and fun, but I have often seen contact with these learning experiences help shy students who are struggling with ballet's formality to "come out of themselves." Many students revel in the spiciness of the rhythms and the special flair of these new movements. Often, hidden personalities are uncovered, and the students return to their classical training with renewed confidence.

CHAPTER 10 *The Recital: To Be or Not to Be?*

*The most practical way of navigating
in the sea of art is to float with the tide.
But if such a course offers you little challenge,
and you wish to choose your own . . . you
can boldly set your course against the tide.*

Mikhail Fokine

Many teachers and owners of music, art, and dance studios feel the need to present an annual show or recital. The main reasons that prompt this decision revolve around public relations and financial benefits. When carefully planned and executed, demonstrations and recitals can provide interesting experiences for students and extra income for the studio. Recitals can also attract new students. However, the primary motivation should not be just to make money, which is often the case.

Many successful studio operators exclude recitals from their curriculum. They find that recitals place extraordinary time and energy demands upon everyone involved. As recital day approaches, activities at the studio often crescendo into chaotic panic. Classes have to be canceled or cut short due to the need for extra rehearsal time during the final weeks of preparation. A great deal of time has to be given to students who are not truly ready for performance. And possibly the most prevalent reason for deciding not to give recitals is that they offer few, if any, genuine artistic benefits.

There are other problems. It is very difficult to gather all participants together at the same time. Volunteer parents (whose involvement is usually essential) often find themselves unable to fulfill the time requirements demanded of them. Students, teachers, and volunteer-parents sometimes become "ill" as recital day approaches. Costumes, props, scenery, and decorations never seem to be ready on time. It is often a problem to locate the appropriate recorded music (live music is usually not a viable option). Jealousies and rivalries sometimes arise among students (and parents), causing tension and occasional temper flare-ups.

However, there is an alternative that fills the artistic void. Instead of an annual recital, consider the following option, which has been used by many teachers with outstanding success. Form a performing group using only your most advanced students, even if there is only a handful who qualify. Compose a written agreement that establishes a list of the specific requirements for participation in this group. Ensure that a copy of this agreement reaches every prospective participant's parents, and have students and parents sign it.

Make sure that this is not a clique of teacher's favorites. It may be necessary to explain to excluded students (and their parents) why they have not been asked to join. Maybe, according to your standards, the student is simply too young. Maybe the student has been missing too many classes lately or is just technically too weak. Maybe there is a weight problem. Or maybe there is a lack of dedication or discipline. Whatever the reason, it is very important to be completely objective and fair. Be sure to let those who have not been selected know that there is a possibility for them to join once they have dealt with the reasons for their exclusion.

Give the group a fitting title such as "(school name) Dance Ensemble." Create a lecture-demonstration program that this group can perform regularly in local area schools, hospitals, civic organizations, and churches. This program might include an audiovisual outline of the history of dance, excerpts from well-known classical ballets, a condensed classroom demonstration, or a demonstration of the correlation between dance training and athletic training. Show how famous athletes have benefited by dance training or how athletic coaches have introduced dance into their training programs. With the dancers participating, end with a lively question-answer session, moderated by a teacher who has a good rapport with the age group that the performance has targeted.

When you return to the studio, gather everyone together and conduct a critique. Invite everyone's participation. Moderate the discussion so it is both positive and objective in analyzing the program. Offer constructive criticism aimed at helping each participant improve. When possible, tape the performance with your video camera so participants can see for themselves how they looked.

The benefits to everyone from this type of learning experience are enormous. It is very likely that such lecture-demonstrations might be the first direct exposure to dance your audiences have experienced. This approach advertises your art and your organization. It also affords your students the opportunity to perform their role as a preprofessional several times during the year, which is vastly superior to the do-or-die, all-or-nothing atmosphere of a one-time annual recital, which is usually performed for an audience of parents and friends.

I have found that many private and public school principals are happy to let you distribute your studio literature to interested students. Naturally, this often attracts new prospects. And if you make certain that your presentations are always of high caliber, your reputation will spread. In addition, you should be able to charge a reasonable honorarium for your demonstration.

This lecture-demonstration approach has two additional benefits. The newer and younger students begin to see the value of earning their way into the dance ensemble, providing an incentive for them to increase the intensity of their own dance practice. And it also causes the students to begin equating hard work and self-discipline with the privilege of performing.

These benefits are distinct from the annual recital, which all too often fosters the idea that performance is a duty (sometimes dreaded) in which everyone is supposed to participate or that performance is a right arising from the mere fact of being enrolled in the school.

In the professional world, public performance opportunities do not come to dancers simply because they put in the time. Not every student can become professionally competent, just as not every competent professional can become a great artist. The master-teacher alerts students to the understanding that performing is a privilege to be earned, stemming from a blend of talent, hard work, and discipline.

CHAPTER 11 *Warming Up and Stretching*

A vision without a task is but a dream,
a task without a vision is drudgery,
a vision with a task is the hope of the world.

Inscription on a church in Sussex,
England, dated 1730 ❧

Most athletic coaches, kinesthesiologists, and doctors advocate warming up before subjecting the body to physical exertion. However, few of these professionals are familiar with the unique stresses that dancing places on the human body.

Many athletic pursuits focus on a narrow range of movements that require acutely focused physical demands. To be prepared for these moments of sudden stress, muscles need to be filled with blood, and all the supporting ligaments and tendons warmed and stretched into a condition of flexibility.

Each type of physical demand on the body has its own warm-up and stretching routine that is appropriate for the type of effort required. The uniqueness of ballet training provides a thoughtfully prepared barre and a center in each daily lesson that incorporate all the warm-up and stretching necessary to prepare the dancers for their daily training event, which is the allegro (jumping) section of the lesson.

The barre and the center exercises, in sequence, act as the dancers' warm-up and the reiteration of important strength-building and coordination-enforcing ingredients. It is the teacher's responsibility to structure each lesson so that students anticipate their "allegro event," an essential ingredient of *every* lesson. A systematic progression of barre and center exercises prepares students' minds and bodies to master an infinite variety of movements, ranging from small, intricate jumps to the most spectacular soaring leaps.

The ambience in the class should stimulate each student's determination to execute barre and center exercises with the utmost skill. The barre begins the warming and stretching process. The center work continues the process and provides the finishing touches for the demands of the allegro combinations. This concept, when understood and correctly executed by knowledgeable teachers, renders warm-ups or stretching routines unnecessary prior to the lesson proper. And it also makes redundant the pre-barre warm-ups and "floor barres" that some teachers employ.

I respect the opinion of those who feel that independent warm-ups before dance lessons are beneficial. I would not argue with such a preference in seasoned dancers who are expected to know their body, how it works, and what it needs. But beginning children and adult students lack such knowledge. We must assume that they do not know much about their bodies at all, and especially how to prepare for the rigors of a dance lesson. While some individuals may be experienced in other spheres of knowledge, that experience does not necessarily prepare them for the unique demands of classical dance. As we continue the discussion of warming up versus stretching, let's assume that we are discussing the issue as it relates to inexperienced students.

As I have previously mentioned, far too many teachers and students either approach dance lessons as preparations for a future event (performance or rehearsal) or treat each segment of a lesson as an event per se. The former believe that the lesson is just a preparation for what will later take place during a rehearsal or onstage. For them the whole lesson is just a warm-up. They do not understand that each lesson should contain elements that will help every participant to improve and get stronger.

The latter believe that they will have a better barre if they warm up and stretch out before the lesson begins. These students often arrive at the studio very early to find a corner to perform their own limbering exercises. A master-teacher's class makes such a routine unnecessary, once one understands that the warming and stretching process that takes place during a well-constructed barre and center is, itself, the preliminary warm-up for the main event—the allegro.

A careful analysis of a well-constructed lesson will bear this out. Imagine a series of slow pliés at the barre that methodically warm up and elongate the ligaments and tendons of the foot, ankle, calf, knee, and hip while simultaneously warming up the thigh, gluteus, and lumbar muscles. This process also impresses upon the mind movement patterns that are repeated throughout the lesson.

Visualize the continuing warm-up sequence as the foot executes first slow, then faster, battements tendus. Then picture what happens to the hip joint and related muscles, ligaments, and tendons while doing slow ronds de jambe par terre and en l'air. Continue analyzing how each set of muscles, ligaments, and tendons is being warmed up and prepared for the center. Then repeat the process, adding complexity to complexity through ever greater demands, as the body is further prepared during the center for the allegro to follow.

This systematic approach is designed to help the body machine produce heat and pliancy and also develop muscle memory. While the muscles are being prepared, the stretchiness induced into the ligaments and tendons gives the needed degree of flexibility to withstand the highly demanding regimen of allegro. And while these physical demands are being placed upon the body, the brain is being prepared to use the muscles automatically.

These brain patterns, called neural engrams, enable dancers to move their bodies without having to be totally concentrated on the mechanics of the movements. These semiautomatic movements free the dancer's mind to concentrate on the choreographic patterns and the emotive and artistic aspects of their performance. The artistic expression expected of a leading dancer or soloist during a performance precludes devoting attention to precisely how or where the body is moving.

Each dance lesson should be designed as a tactic in the overall strategy to prepare students for their ultimate goal, the performance on stage. The body must be systematically conditioned for that purpose. This systematic conditioning includes alternating the physical demand from small muscle groups to larger ones. It also incorporates carefully designed lifting-emphasis exercises to develop strength, such as battements développés and relevés lents, while other exercises emphasize either quickness or maybe plasticity. Still other exercises are incorporated to promote equilibrium and balance control, even in the most complex movements and occasionally awkward positions.

A well-organized training curriculum creates stretching exercises that enable dancers to adopt even the most radical postures, such as controlled leg extensions—the big poses and grands battements. Also included are exercises that methodically warm up the entire arm, from shoulder to fingertip, using a variety of port de bras. And, finally, students must learn how to coordinate all the muscle groups used in exercises that prepare the dancer for jumping. Some of these are battement fondu, grand battement jeté, tombé, coupé, and frappé.

In the beginning, students perform the above exercises by holding onto the barre, either with one hand or both. Later, many of these same exercises are repeated in the center where greater challenges are added, such as static balance (demi-pointe), rotating balance (pirouettes), and shifting balance (changes from one leg to the other).

Finally, after repeatedly meeting these challenges, the body and mind are ready to add the ultimate challenge, *levitation*. Dancers' confrontation with gravity is their most demanding test. The goal of the soaring leap is to free the dancer from subservience to the gravitational pulls of the earth.

Levitation also places extraordinary emphasis on unique breathing practices. It requires great stamina to push beyond one's perceived limitations. And jumping demands that each student learn how to interact successfully with pain (discussed in chapter 5).

This brings us back to our original question, Do dancers really need a prelesson warm-up? Some people derive a psychological boost from preclass preparations. In that sense, the prelesson warm-up may be beneficial, if it truly helps the students feel that they are better prepared for the lesson. As you can see, these questions raise questions requiring thoughtful consideration and astute judgment by teachers.

I have found that the most important prelesson preparation for a student, or professional dancer for that matter, is the preparation of thought. It is important to begin each lesson with single-minded focus. Therefore, students should arrive at the studio early. While changing from street clothing to ballet attire, they should make a conscious effort to discard all distracting cares, and enter into the "dancerly paradigm," the psychological state of mind that promotes progress. I reiterate that a disciplined mental effort is required to rid the mind of mundane distractions that divert students from making the daily lesson a constructive learning experience. Students who practice this preclass routine over time invariably begin to display an extraordinary level of self-discipline, receptivity, and accurate retentiveness of what they are learning.

CONSTRUCTIVE WARM-UP

Decades of study and research by experts have provided the following valuable rule-of-thumb: Warm up at the start; stretch out at the end.

Warming up and stretching are different activities that serve quite different functions. Warming up is accomplished primarily through repeated muscle flexions and releases, including very small movements, such as repetitively alternating between pointing the foot forward and flexing it backward. The following exercises may be done while lying on the floor:

EXAMPLE 1. Rotate the ankles in *wide* circles, both quickly and slowly, and outward and inward.

EXAMPLE 2. Variations on the theme of sit-ups or curl-ups (often called "crunches") with knees bent and without holding the feet down. Strengthening the entire abdominal girdle is necessary for good control of TBS.

EXAMPLE 3. Raising the shoulders from the floor while lying on the stomach.

Other exercises, such as the following, may be done while seated in a chair:

EXAMPLE 1. Bending and straightening the knees while the thigh muscles hold the upper leg steady.

EXAMPLE 2. Rotate the head and neck in *wide* circles in both directions.

EXAMPLE 3. Elongate the neck vertically, then try to touch the top of the left shoulder with the left ear, and the same with the right.

EXAMPLE 4. With the arms extended straight forward at shoulder height, rotate them in circles, first away from each other, then toward each other.

EXAMPLE 5. With the arms extended straight to the side at shoulder height, rotate them in small circles in both directions.

There are also exercises, such as the following, that can be done while standing:

EXAMPLE 1. Bend the torso sideways with the opposing arm raised overhead (for example, right arm up—bend left).

EXAMPLE 2. Bend the torso forward and backward and around a circle.

EXAMPLE 3. With shoulders isolated, rotate them in circles forward and backward.

The above warm-ups attract and circulate blood to the entire body. They also attune the students' minds to the lesson's first exercise.

In contrast, many students and professionals can be observed engaging in such counterproductive measures as the often-seen, bouncing stretch of ice-cold muscles, ligaments, and tendons before class. Their rationale is that such stretches help them feel loose during the lesson. I have cringed many times on seeing professionals (who should know better) walk out of the dressing room and drop suddenly into a split followed by a series of yanks and jerks of cold limbs. This mindless activity overstretches and strains muscle fibers and connective tissues. *Ouch!*

Overstretching is read by the affected part of the brain as a threatening activity. The brain then causes the "attacked" muscle fibers to contract automatically—their natural response to such twinges of pain. Though mild, the pain is real, but the stress is not severe enough to be considered an injury—*yet.* However, each such twinge is an injury in the making.

Ignorant dancers respond to such twinges by favoring the overstretched body part during subsequent lessons, which places even greater stress on other areas of the body. Sometimes dancers respond by stretching the area even more as the area's contracting muscles and tissues begin to stiffen and feel tight. This latter course of action releases endorphins in the brain that momentarily, at least partially, relieve the pain. And as long as the body is kept warm and moving, the dancer can usually continue working. However, the continued stretching of such an injured area usually ends in pulls or strains and the potential for major problems such as chronic tendonitis.

Dancers who persist in the cyclical sequence of preclass stretching to relieve tightness → twinges → muscle contractions → recurring tightness → leading to more stretching almost assuredly will develop chronic disabilities. To counteract the pain, dancers sometimes resort to pain-killing drugs. It is sad to see professionals trapped in this vicious cycle throughout their careers, dancing in almost constant pain. The result is often premature retirement to a sometimes tragic and unnecessary semi-invalidism. Teachers, ballet masters, and company directors can spare their dancers this lifelong misery by being better informed.

In sum, cold muscles, ligaments, and tendons are not ready for heavy stretching! Have students who feel the need to stretch do so after the lesson is over and their bodies are well warmed up. And be sure to show them how to do it properly! For example, show them how to stretch to approximately 80 percent of the body part's maximum muscular elongation, hold for three to five seconds, and relax for two or three seconds. Then they can repeat the sequence at 90 percent and then at just under 100 percent of the body's natural stretch limit.

The next step might be to repeat the same procedure holding the stretched body part for eight to ten seconds, beginning again with the 80 percent stretch and working up gradually to 100 percent (the dancer's limit). Finally, repeat the sequence as above ending with a stretch to slightly beyond the body's natural limit. Dancers should use this sequence for each major muscle group.

Breathing correctly is extremely important while executing the above stretches. Always *inhale before* beginning the stretch. Then slowly and deeply *exhale during* the stretching movement.

Although my experience indicates that there is no physiological need to have students help one another stretch, I have observed good results from the spirit of camaraderie that often arises from this practice. Students participating in such activities must, however, be *closely* monitored. I advise teachers to oversee new assistant teachers who permit or suggest stretching, since I have witnessed such horrors as allowing students to stand on each other's bent knees while lying on the floor, to promote turnout; and allowing them to put their entire weight on top of the insteps to make the feet point better.

The worst that can happen to students who do not warm the muscles before class is that they will be forced to rely on the completeness of the teacher's lesson for the warming process. This is not a problem with a master-teacher's lesson. But students who prestretch the ligaments and tendons improperly, or too forcefully, may one day find themselves carried out of class or rehearsal on a stretcher to a waiting ambulance, due to a knee slipping out of joint or to torn ligaments. Tendonitis, stress fractures, and chronic strains have prematurely ended many promising careers or have resulted in radical surgical processes, such as hip replacements, in later life.

This subject requires vigilance on the part of every teacher, ballet master, and company director.

CHAPTER 12

Belonging and Contributing

Through art humanity is civilized.
Through dance humanity is vitalized.

Anonymous

Joining organizations that promote the exchange of new ideas, attending seminars to learn new concepts and discuss mutual problems, and subscribing to trade journals are ways for serious teachers to keep abreast of their field. But since there are many avenues to choose from, one must be selective. What criteria should be used in making such selections?

I have found it useful to scrutinize what the prospective organization or publication advocates. Ask yourself the following questions: Do they perpetuate the status quo, elitism, trendiness, or mediocrity? Or do they emphasize high standards of excellence? What are the professional credentials of the people in charge? Do those in charge deal predominantly with the artistic side of dance? the technical side? or a balanced approach? Is it possible to gain professional expertise through association with the organization? It is wise to be persistent in answering these questions.

Some organizations are primarily based upon making money. They are run by businesspeople who promote the idea that bigger is better. In these organizations there is little, if any, emphasis on the *art* of dance. If one aspires to be a true master-teacher, it is essential to search out organizations that provide a genuine service to the art, whose mission and goals are based upon elevating the quality of dance education. You may derive a legitimate benefit from such associations and feel part of the dance community. I also urge such organizations to share their knowledge and expertise when it is sought by responsible colleagues and novice teachers.

I have seen remarkable progress by students and teachers who study and apply the principles of the Vaganova syllabus. The information is widely available, but due to its complexity, the highest levels of achievement can be derived only from close association with a master-teacher who has been thoroughly trained in teaching the method. Attaining real expertise is virtually impossible through independent study. There are just too many complexities and too many subtle details requiring explanation by an authority.

Consider visiting ballet centers of the former Soviet Union as a focus for a working vacation. Be aware that the administration and staff of these schools nearly always try to show their best work by allowing visitors to observe only specially prepared demonstration classes. To gain access to regular daily lessons visitors must convince the authorities of their seriousness and dedication to classical tradition.

Another way to learn is to attend one of the many national or international dance competitions, such as those held in Varna, Bulgaria; Moscow, Russia; Paris, France; Helsinki, Finland; Japan; and Jackson, Mississippi. Schedule your time to arrive a day or two early and remain a day or two after the official competition has ended. This gives you time to meet colleagues and compare notes on an informal basis. Keep in mind that many of the competitors and their coaches have traveled thousands of miles to get there, so it is unlikely that you will have an opportunity to meet them again unless you have the means and are free to travel extensively.

On these trips I suggest that you take along a good quality video camera and plenty of tapes. In conjunction with this, it is wise to begin your own video library, which can enhance your own teaching in the absence of a regular association with a master-teacher. The videos can also serve as a reminder of what high-quality dance should be like and can be useful teaching aids when shown to your students.

Another way to pursue your study is to budget time to observe classes of known master-teachers in cities you are visiting. Visit their studios, and invite them to visit you when they come to your area. Try to find something in common apart from dance that will open the door to regular exchanges of phone calls and letters.

Another avenue for expanding your professional contacts is to arrange to visit the headquarters of ballet companies that are located in cities you plan to visit. However—a caveat—keep in mind that a company's "professional" reputation does not ensure that classes are well structured or well taught. In fact, some company directors consider classes to be only warm-ups for rehearsals or performances. Surprisingly, there are not many directors or ballet masters who have received formal training from master-teachers in teaching well-designed ballet lessons. Many feel that their own dancing experience is sufficient preparation for them to run a company and teach.

Classes offered in schools associated with professional companies are also sometimes sadly lacking in direction and organization. Company schools are in a position to attract students due to their association with the parent company, but students and parents are urged to carefully scrutinize *all* schools before enrolling. A school's association with a company does not ensure quality dance instruction.

These suggestions are offered to help serious teachers expand their horizons. There is a vast difference between artistic professionalism and the level of instruction that pays more attention to commercial issues. Schools that enroll hundreds, even thousands, of students of all ages and abilities in a curriculum that combines ballet, jazz, tap, and hula into a single class may provide their owners with lucrative year-end recitals, costume sales, coaching fees, photo sessions, competitions, conventions, and so forth. But they are not contributors to the art of dance. By now, the reader will have realized that this book is concerned with the art of classical ballet, with excellence, and with improving the quality of dance education.

Sending students to dance-convention extravaganzas, where hundreds of students gather to compete for trophies and take lessons with "name" teachers, is minimally beneficial for students and teachers. Even the most perceptive teacher cannot offer significant help to such a conglomeration of ages and abilities. Most genuine master-teachers avoid such enterprises.

If you feel it is important for your students to experience taking lessons with other teachers, invite a guest teacher to teach in your studio for a week or two. A longer period would be even better. Guest teachers worthy of the name master-teacher will want to spend time to get to know your students, so they can give them some real help. By observing such teachers at work, you will almost certainly be able to incorporate some ideas that will improve your skills.

We have seen that mixing different teaching methods or dance styles in the early years of a student's training is not advisable. I am aware that some teachers believe that this approach allows students to experience a variety of methods and new ideas. However, my more than thirty years of teaching and observation have led me to conclude that, in the long run, such an approach ends in confusion and dissipation of focus.

Additionally, if you frequently attend seminars on various teaching methods, your own system can become confused. It takes many years to gain in-depth understanding of a single method. Comprehending the tenets of a method provides clarity and logic to the system. Don't be in a hurry to exact change. First, prove all the components of the method you have chosen to work with. Then try to determine whether or not your ideas for change would be valid improvements. I can report that during my years working with the Vaganova method, I have not yet found areas that need improvement. I base my judgment on the extremely high quality of dancers, products of the method, who have impressed the world for decades with their extraordinary technical and artistic abilities. Occasionally I hear protests to the contrary, but these usually come from people who have had only superficial experiences with the intricacies of the Vaganova system.

Finally, a smorgasbord sampling often puts you in the position of judging which is best or correct. Some existing theories are incompatible with each other. Only true master-teachers have the knowledge and experience to discern the differences and make critical judgments, and even then they should do so with great care. Long-established principles that have been refined over a period of decades should not be easily dismissed, especially if they are not thoroughly understood.

Occasionally, master-teachers might have the experience and knowledge to formulate new ideas or modify established ones, based on their years of dancing, study, observation, or teaching. Before developing innovative new theories or attempting to improve on established concepts, I have found it best to first master a method, such as Mme. Vaganova's, that has a long history of proven results. Mastery of a method makes you feel that you own the method—that it is part of your unique understanding. This mastery provides a foundation on which to explore new avenues and continue growing. Remember, your students' successes are a mirror of your teaching ability.

Mutual support is essential to the perpetual advancement of the art. Let's be determined to exclude from our experience any atmosphere of envy or rivalry that would try to undermine and destroy the beauty of our art. If we dedicate ourselves to becoming the best teachers we can be, to study, to learn our trade, and above all, to strive for excellence, we can honestly say that we are contributors to one of the most exciting performing arts bequeathed to us by our illustrious predecessors.

"Dance is communication, and so the great challenge is to speak clearly, beautifully, and with inevitability," said Martha Graham. Fellow teachers, we have chosen the part of our art that requires the greatest responsibility—to pass on to future generations the knowledge and traditions that have become an integral part of our lives. Let us help our students "speak," as Miss Graham has said, "with inevitability." Master-teachers are committed to this end. Our art depends on it.

APPENDIX A   *Vaganova Syllabus Épaulement and Direction Diagram*

With the dancer standing in the center of an imaginary square, the position *en face* is directed toward point 1 (the audience or mirror). The basic big and small poses that incorporate épaulement (the plane of the body created by the shoulders, hips, and feet) are directed at 45 degree angles toward points 2 and 8. The other points of the square are given to help guide the directions of poses that the dancer executes en tournant and along the diagonals. Teachers must see that students memorize this concept so they do not use the walls and corners of the room as points of reference, because these points may not correctly divide directions into proper angles.

FIGURE 16   *Vaganova Syllabus direction diagram*

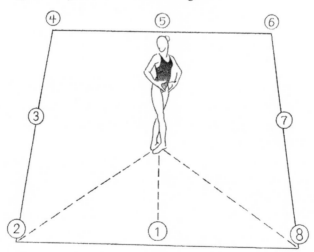

An Advanced Lesson Outline

---

*The purpose for dance class is to make
the interior more visible.*

Alvin Ailey

The following guidelines for an advanced classical dance lesson incorporate the principles of this teaching manual. It is not meant to be a complete lesson plan. It is a general outline in which specifics are not detailed, leaving ample room for knowledgeable teachers to inject ideas of their own. This outline is for a typical 90-minute lesson. After a preliminary révérence, the lesson begins as follows:

BARRE

1. Simple combination of demi-plié and grand plié, in first, second, fourth, and fifth positions combined with simple port de bras.
2. Battement tendu with and without plié.
3. Battement tendu jeté.
4. Rond de jambe par terre with more complex port de bras.
5. Battement fondu (or battement soutenu) on the whole foot and on demi-pointe.
6. Battement frappé and battement double frappé on the whole foot and on demi-pointe.
7. Rond de jambe and double rond de jambe en l'air on the whole foot and on demi-pointe.

8. Petit battement sur le cou-de-pied and battement battu on demi-pointe.
9. Adagio comprising a variety of big poses and complex transitions from pose to pose.
10. Grand battement jeté.

OPTIONAL

1. Additional relevés; or
2. Additional pas de bourrées; or
3. Battements pour batterie.

Many of the above exercises should end with a half turn (without stopping the music) and continue on the other side. Where appropriate, barre exercises should be done with épaulement using small and big poses.

BARRE COMBINATIONS

1. Exercises 5 and 6 above can be combined into a single exercise.
2. Using appropriate musical transitions, exercises 7 and 8 can be combined into a single exercise.
3. Many barre exercises can be speeded up through the use of half and whole turns on one or both legs.
4. Exercises and combinations can be enriched through the use of various connecting steps such as tombé-coupé, pas de bourrée, flic-flac, temps relevé, fouetté, and tours (pirouettes).

The above exercises, and combination-exercises, follow a general pattern of alternation between slow/fast and heavy/light. This guideline is extremely important because it helps to prevent fatiguing the muscles or building bulky musculature.

This barre should be kept moving at a brisk pace, so it can be completed in no more than 25 to 30 minutes. Accomplished professionals can get through a complete barre in about 20 minutes. When the barre is done at a brisk pace, your students will be adequately warmed up for the center exercises that follow.

Notice how I phrased the foregoing, "warmed up for the center exercises that follow." This warm-up is important in planning a lesson that will be of maximum benefit to your students.

CENTER

In general, the elements and sequence of center exercises should be related to those studied at the barre. Center exercises also add four new elements that teachers should stress:

1. The demand for unsupported balance—*insist* that students' minds are focused upon elegant aplomb and equipoise.
2. Turns of all kinds.
3. An expanded use of épaulement and demi-pointe.
4. Greater use of the "language" of poses, and smooth transitions from one to another.

The following should be included in the center exercises of all advanced lessons:

1. A short adagio comprised of demi-pliés blended with slow work in the big poses (croisés, effacés, écartés, arabesques, and attitudes).
2. Battement tendu or temps lié combinations.
3. Battement fondu or battement soutenu combinations.
4. A grand adagio comprised of more complex and lengthy use of poses, tours lents, pirouettes in big poses, renversé, penché, ballotté, grand plié, and jumps in isolation.
5. Grand battement jeté.

Tours sur le cou-de-pied and pirouettes in big poses should be incorporated into most of the above exercises. They should be designed to have a character that matches the style of the combination; for example, tours sur le cou-de-pied en dehors and en dedans fit well into exercises 2 and 3 above, whereas pirouettes in big poses blend well with exercise 4. In addition, students should be taught that most types of pirouettes must be learned in both allegro and adagio style. In other words, the dynamics of the tour must fit the mood and tempo of the music and the design of the choreography.

The small and large poses incorporating épaulement should be used with increased frequency. And many exercises are done on demi-pointe and en tournant. Also, exercises should be designed so that they can be reversed. A well-designed curriculum covers *all* of the poses, and *all* of the various tours (pirouettes), during each six- to eight-week period.

Finally, do not specialize! Do not spend extra time on steps or combinations that are your favorites. It is important that you cover all the material.

The center section of the lesson should last approximately 40 to 45 minutes, except on the days when you intend to give the girls pointe at the end of the lesson. Remember, it is more beneficial to give pointe for 15 or 20 minutes every day than to give a pointe lesson once or twice a week. By the time the center work is completed, the students should be thoroughly warmed up and ready to jump. The pace should be fast, as it was during the barre.

ALLEGRO

The allegro section of the lesson should include the following:

1. Simple jumps from two legs (changement and échappé).
2. Simple jumps from two legs onto one leg (simple sissonne), from one leg onto one (jeté, ballonné), and from one leg onto two (assemblé).
3. Simple beats (royale, échappé battu, entrechat quatre).
4. Middle jumps (sissonne fermée, sissonne ouverte).
5. Grand allegro (various).
6. Complex beats (cabriole, entrechat six, brisé volé).
7. Small jumps at a fast tempo.
8. Port de bras and révérence.

Teachers are free to introduce a wide variety of steps during the allegro. The entire allegro curriculum indicated in the syllabus for the year should be covered and repeated often so it is well understood and fixed in the muscle memory.

Nearly all allegro combinations should be studied equally on both sides and reversed. If a combination is executed forwards on both sides, it should then be executed backwards on both sides to the original starting position (or with a change of feet to repeat the exercise from the other side).

On days when the girls are scheduled for pointe, have them retire to change shoes after doing not fewer than three allegro exercises. While the girls are changing shoes, work with the boys in the class, according to their ability, on the typically masculine steps such as tours en l'air, double saut de basque, cabrioles in big poses, entrechat six, grande sissonne ouverte, and consecutive pirouettes à la seconde.

The above outline provides a format for lessons at the advanced level. It also allows a great deal of individual discretion. This systematic approach to teaching methodology is time-tested. It has consistently proved that it results in technically strong and professionally capable dancers.

FIGURE 17 *Positions of the arms*

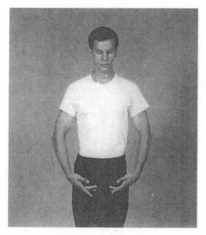

Preparatory pose.　　　　　　First position.

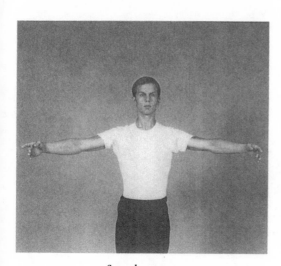

Second position.　　　　　　Third position.

FIGURE 18 *Positions of the feet*

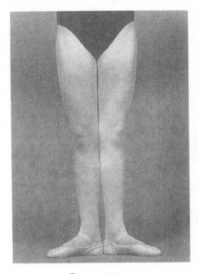

First position.

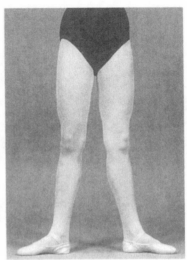

Second position.

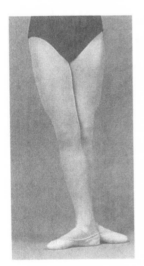

Third position.

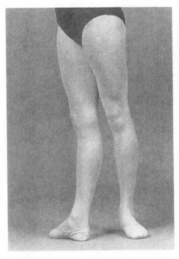

Fourth position (feet are an extension
of fifth position, not third position,
i.e., heel of the front foot is aligned
with the toes of the back foot).

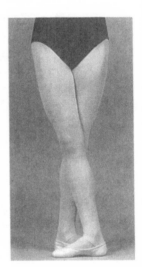

Fifth position.

FIGURE 19 *Correct hands*

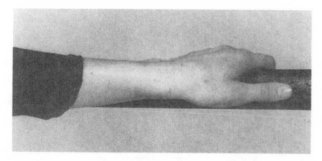

On the barre.

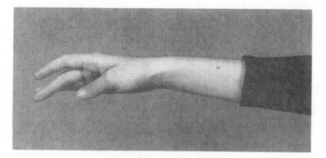

Palm facing down.

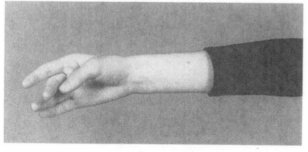

Palm facing forward.

FIGURE 2 0 *Épaulement*

 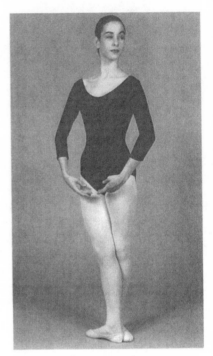

Épaulement croisé.   *Épaulement effacé.*

FIGURE 21 *Poses croisés*

Small pose devant.

Big pose devant.

Small pose derrière.

Big pose derrière.

FIGURE 22 *Poses effacés*

Small pose devant.

Big pose devant.

Small pose derrière.

Big pose derrière.

FIGURE 23 *Poses écartés.*

Small pose devant.

Big pose devant.

Small pose derrière.

Big pose derrière.

FIGURE 24 *Arabesques*

First arabesque.

Second arabesque.

FIGURE 25 *Attitudes*

Croisé devant.

Croisé derrière.

Third arabesque.

Fourth arabesque.

Effacé derrière.

FIGURE 26   *Positions of the foot sur le cou-de-pied and retiré*

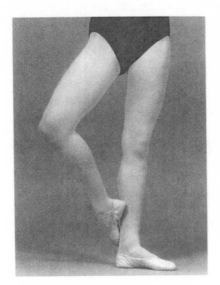

Basic position.

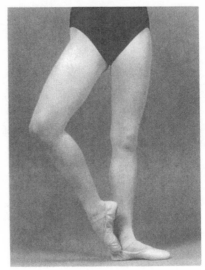

Low conditional position.

Conditional position.

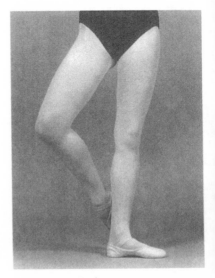

Back position.

Retiré devant.

Retiré derrière.

FIGURE 27

*Position of the foot
during passé*

FIGURE 28   *The first port de bras*

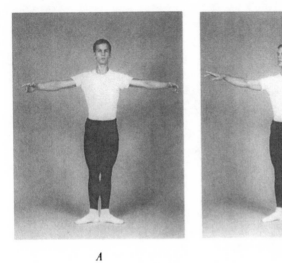

A   B   C

FIGURE 29   *The second port de bras*

A   B   C

D   *E*   *F*

D   *E*   *F*

FIGURE 30   *The third port de bras*

A

B

E

C

D

F

G

FIGURE 31   *The fourth port de bras*

A

B

E

C   D

F   G

FIGURE 32   *The fifth port de bras*

A   B   C

D   E

FIGURE 33   *The sixth port de bras*

A

B

E

F

C   D

G   H   I

FIGURE 34   *Cambré at the barre*

To the side.   To the back.

APPENDIX C *Bits and Pieces*

A true performing artist exerts willpower upon the
*audience; bears a **forceful** presence; does not say,*
*"Please watch me" courteously, but **demands**,*
*"Now you **pay attention** here!"*

Itzhak Perlman

The following is a collage of some guidelines and observations that I have
assembled during my years of teaching, coaching, and pedagogical study.
These tidbits of useful information are listed in random order with no im-
plied ranking of importance. I am certain that many of my colleagues could
add to this list. All the information is directly related to the pursuit of excellence. Some tidbits relate to the application of the Vaganova syllabus. The
reader will find that many have already been incorporated into the text of this
book. These are reiterated because of their importance.

1. Exercises at the barre should be *well* executed to the side before being done
   forward and backward.

2. Don't become a slave of the en croix habit. Instead, after doing a movement front-side-back, do a port de bras or hold a pose for the equivalent
   remaining music time. Then reverse the whole exercise (back-side-front,
   port de bras or pose). This routine provides an equal number of repetitions in each direction and also allows for practice of other essential ingredients.

3. Everting (bending toward the outside of the leg) the foot at the ankle,
   often seen in arabesque and attitude poses, weakens the ankle, making

the dancer vulnerable to injury. The foot should be evenly stretched (pointed) at all times.

4. The head and eyes should always accompany a port de bras.

5. Except for beginning students, it is not necessary to use preparatory arm positioning before exercises that incorporate a port de bras as an integral part of the movement (for example, battement fondu or battement développé). A preparatory port de bras for such movements is redundant.

6. For beginning students, exercises should be combined or complicated only after simple versions are thoroughly assimilated.

7. When repeating certain movements several times in a row, such as battement tendu jeté or battement frappé, use an odd number (e.g., 3, 5, 7) of repetitions for each series. This method creates a pause within the musical phrase, providing a clearly defined conclusion to each repeating series of movements while giving the mind an opportunity to shift gears during the pause, before the legs are required to change direction. This is a very useful teaching device.

8. It is more constructive to teach exercises using the same working leg several times in a row, rather than alternating legs. Not only do the legs receive a more thorough workout and build muscle memory, but the mind can focus more acutely since it does not have to cope with continuous changes.

9. Aplomb (vertical stability) is developed in the center through the use of demi-pointe, turns, and changes from one leg to the other.

10. Overcoming the difficulty of controlling balances is made easier through frequent work on demi-pointe, which forces students to pull themselves together. Always work on high demi-pointe. Dancing on low demi-pointe overworks the calf muscle.

11. Plié is a movement, *not* a pose.

12. During petit changement de pied, the legs should open slightly when taking off from the floor. During grand changement de pied, keep the legs together in fifth position during the takeoff. Then, during the descent, change the legs. The same rule applies to échappés to second and fourth positions.

13. Assemblé should close the legs into fifth position precisely at the apex of the jump.

14. Beats during all entrechats, cabrioles, and battu versions of steps should happen at the apex of the jump. This is the body's quietest moment when the audience can see the beat most clearly.

15. Giving pointe segments as a part of each regular lesson helps students accept pointe work as a normal part of their training. Separate pointe classes (which are physically harder on students) then become unnecessary.

16. Begin each exercise with a four-measure musical introduction instead of the familiar two chords. Hearing the quality and tempo of the musical introduction helps students begin their movements in a dynamic and positive manner.

17. Do not be a dabbler, picking and choosing what you think is best among the various teaching methods. Instead, become an expert on the one that suits your needs.

18. Don't be afraid to make radical changes in your teaching methods if you discover ways to improve your skills. Just tell your students that from now on they are going to do things differently. They will adapt.

19. Try to convince students (and their parents) that attending classes regularly and often is the only way to learn to dance, regardless of natural ability and talent.

20. Begin and end each exercise cleanly and with authority.

21. Complete dancers are created by complete teachers.

22. Complications added haphazardly = confusion. Complications added in logical sequence = enrichment. When students are ready, adding complexities to simple movements is an extension of the fundamentals necessary to develop complete dancers.

23. Starting students in classical ballet training before the age of eight results in spending excessive time on noncurriculum coordination and discipline. The short attention span of very young students will tempt teachers to compromise and skip over important details.

24. Exercises in the center that are executed en face look more finished when they begin and end with épaulement croisé.

25. Passé is not a pose or a position. It is a movement that happens when the working leg passes by the side of the supporting leg while en route from one pose to another.

26. Coupé is not a pose or a position. It is a movement that "cuts" one foot away

from the other. It is usually done as a preparation for another step, as in coupé-assemblé. Coupé is often mistakenly confused with the term *cou-de-pied*. When a foot is placed on the ankle of the other leg, the working foot is said to be "sur le cou-de-pied" (literally, "on the neck of the foot").

27. Battement battu is a lateral in-and-out movement, done either in front of or in back of the supporting ankle, not an up-and-down movement.

28. When doing a series of quick small jumps in succession, épaulement should not be used. However, the head continues to turn toward the front shoulder in accordance with the rules for the given step.

29. Begin teaching grand plié to beginners in the middle of the barre exercise, following rond de jambe par terre. Introduce it approximately halfway through the first year to students who are studying every day. For students who come less frequently, wait until the end of the year.

30. Grand plié is a continuous movement. There should be no pause at the bottom. It is easier to begin grand plié in second position, but it is more instructive for students to learn to control the movement when starting in first position.

31. The term *technique* generally refers to the controlled and coordinated use of the legs and feet. Artistic qualities are expressed through the use of the head, eyes, arms, and hands.

32. Tombé is a preliminary exercise for learning grand jeté.
    a) Rise to demi-pointe on the supporting leg;
    b) extend the working leg;
    c) lift and carry the hips in the direction of the tombé (literally, fall);
    d) transfer the body weight to a point just beyond the toes of the outstretched working leg.

33. Students should not be allowed to keep their eyes focused on themselves in the mirror. The eyes must change their point of focus in conjunction with the épaulement and pose given. The eyes should always look straight out at eye level in the direction established by the turned head. An exception to this rule is the poses écartés, when the head and eyes incline slightly upward or downward to match the alignment of the inclined torso.

34. *Battement* is a ballet term describing a movement involving the opening *and* closing of the working leg. *Dégagé* is the opening portion of a battement.

35. Beyond the beginning level, a complete lesson should *always* include a grand adagio in the center and no less than three allegro combinations.

36. It is appropriate to establish rules to help students learn the precise details for every movement or pose. Later, advanced students learn that there are variations on these patterns that can be used within the decorums of good taste and classical tradition.

37. Most individual movements should be attacked on the strong accent of the musical phrase, which provides a natural, dynamic emphasis. Musical signatures have certain beats that are stronger than others (for example, beat 1 of a 3/4 measure, or beats 1 and 3 of a 4/4 measure). When movements are executed on these strong accents they seem to make sense and have a kinetic coordination between the eyes that see the movement and the ears that hear the accompanying music. Using the music in this way will make your combinations seem more logical, lyrical, and musical. I recommend that all teachers give this concept considerable thought.

38. Teach your students to *dance the music* or *become the music*, rather than simply dance *to* the music.

39. The following are the main features of Vaganova's method of teaching classical ballet:

   a) The "holding" of the lower back and stomach, resulting in overall strength of the trunk and a positive connection between the upper body and the legs;

   b) the use of the arms in precise forms;

   c) the division of the small and big poses;

   d) the use of the head and eyes in épaulement;

   e) studying all movements (except some tours) by a systematic progression through various forms;

   f) the precise musical breakdown of each exercise;

   g) a complete awareness of the direct link between the mind and the body (development of artistry).

40. Working with a proven curriculum, such as the Vaganova syllabus, helps to eliminate many commonly found chronic problems, for example, poor placement, weakness of the stomach and lower back, and the inability to coordinate arm and head movement with the legs and feet.

41. In any endeavor, never be intimidated by another's ability or success. Be-

cause someone else's light seems to shine more brightly than your own does not mean that you must live in their shadow. And you need not compete for another's light. Discover and radiate your own.

42. Regarding innovation, Vaganova wrote in an article, "Pupils who have not seen me for a long time find an improvement and progress in my teaching. What is the cause of this? Look at life all around; everything is growing, everything is moving forward. Therefore, I recommend . . . keeping in touch with life and with art."

43. Alexander Gorsky, former artistic director of the Bolshoi Ballet Company, once said, "If the dancer is negligent about the artistic side of his work during class, it will be difficult for him to show artistry when he later dances."

44. Vaganova's assistant teacher, Vera Kostrovitskaya, wrote about her mentor, "By the words, 'development of technique,' we do not imply work only on swift chaînés, a great number of fouettés, or the like. For it is possible to speak of a real technique of execution only when the body, arms and head of the dancer become the means by which the language of dance is expressed and are responsive to every emotion."

45. Great artistic heights are only achieved through hard work, discipline and motivation.

46. Emphasis on the organic quality of movement (feeling) at the expense of technique promotes instability and confusion. The audience should never have to worry about whether or not a dancer will be able to successfully complete the task. Technical proficiency leads to artistic freedom.

47. The development of talent is primarily accomplished by exercising the "muscle" between the ears. A beautifully pointed foot and a high arabesque are not signs of talent.

48. Struggle for perfection, and never be afraid of making mistakes.

49. On giving scholarships—the rewards of those who pay for the services they require are far sweeter than those that are generously given to an ingrate. Carefully evaluate potential scholarship recipients.

50. The beauty of one's art is not meant to be held within. It is meant to be expressed openly and joyfully.

51. Above all else, *excellence!*

Organization of Former Soviet Ballet Schools

At the time of the breakup of the Soviet Union there were twenty state choreographic schools among the republics. There were no private dancing schools, as we know them. However, dance instruction was offered in culture and recreation centers often connected with centers of work and the Young Pioneers (a communist youth organization). A wide range of activities was available to all interested students. The classical ballet curriculum taught in these centers (similar to our YMCAS and recreation centers) followed the basics of the Vaganova methodology, which is the system used exclusively throughout all the republics.

Enrollment in one of the state schools is extremely competitive, and it is considered a great privilege to be accepted. Students begin between the ages of nine or ten, and graduate at about the age of eighteen. All teachers in the state schools use the Vaganova syllabus. The syllabus is divided into eight grades or classes. Each class has a specifically prescribed curriculum-plan for the year, and the assigned teacher is expected to cover all the indicated material.

Dance students in state schools are carefully screened to ensure that they meet at least minimum prescribed physical and psychological requirements. Once accepted into a choreographic school, they are required to attend dance lessons daily, six days per week. Students enrolled in these state schools usually reside in school housing facilities and are given primary and secondary education along with their ballet training.

In addition to the regular eight-year program of study, some former Soviet ballet academies have, in the past, experimented with a special six-year program for older beginning students, twelve to fourteen years of age, who were exceptionally talented and showed clear professional potential. Natalia Makarova was a notable graduate of this special program at the Vaganova Choreographic School in Leningrad (now St. Petersburg). In the six-year syllabus, the elementary work of the first three years of the regular program was done in two years, and the intermediate work of the fourth, fifth, and sixth years of the regular program was also done in two years. In this way, the fourth class of the six-year program became essentially the same as the sixth class of the eight-year program. The final two years were essentially identical.

Originally the Vaganova method was a nine-year program. It was shortened to eight years in the 1960s. Beginning students at that time were between eight and nine years of age. Very little new material was introduced during the ninth year. It was considered a final year for polishing and consolidating and to help the dancer establish individuality.

Bibliography

Barnes, Patricia, and Earle Mack. *Children of Theatre Street*. New York: Penguin Books, 1978.

Bazarova, Nadezhda, and Varvara Mey. *Alphabet of Classical Dance*. Leningrad, 1983, and London: Dance Books, 1987.

Blasis, Carlo. *An Elementary Treatise upon the Theory and Practice of the Art of Dancing*. New York: Kamin Dance Gallery, 1944.

Golovkina, Sofia. *Lessons in Classical Dance*. London: Dance Books, 1991.

Grant, Gail. *Technical Manual and Dictionary of Classical Ballet*. New York: Dover Publications, 1967.

Grieg, Valerie. *Inside Ballet Technique*. Princeton, N.J.: Princeton Book Co., 1994.

Kahn, Albert E. *Days with Ulanova*. New York: Simon and Schuster, 1962.

Kostrovitskaya, Vera. *101 Classical Dance Lessons*. Leningrad: Iskusstvo, 1972. Translated by John Barker. New York: privately printed, 1979.

Kostrovitskaya, Vera, and Alexei Pisarev. *School of Classical Dance*. Moscow: Progress, 1978.

Messerer, Asaf. *Classes in Classical Ballet*. Moscow: Iskusstvo, 1967. Translated by Oleg Briansky. New York: Doubleday, 1975.

Morley, Iris. *Soviet Ballet*. London: Collins Press, 1946.

Morton, Miriam. *The Arts and the Soviet Child*. New York: The Free Press, 1972.

Roslavleva, Natalia. *Era of the Russian Ballet*. New York: E. P. Dutton and Co., 1966.

Serebrennikov, Nicolai. *The Art of Pas de Deux*. Moscow: 1969, and London: Dance Books, 1978.

Slonimsky, Juri, et al. *The Soviet Ballet*. New York: Philosophical Library, 1947.

Stanislavski, Konstantine. *My Life in Art*. New York: Meridian Books, 1956.

Tarasov, Nikolai. *Ballet Technique for the Male Dancer*. Moscow: 1971.

Vaganova, Agrippina. *Basic Principles of Classical Ballet*. New York: Dover Publications, 1969.

Index

JOHN WHITE is codirector of the Pennsylvania Academy of Ballet, located in a Philadelphia suburb, which he opened with his wife in 1974. He has been a soloist and the ballet master of the Ballet Nacional de Cuba and the head instructor and interim ballet master of the Pennsylvania Ballet Company. Since 1980 he has conducted seminars for dance teachers, training more than 400 teachers during this time. He has also been a contributing editor and writer for *Ballet Dancer Magazine*.

CPSIA information can be obtained at www.ICGtesting.com
Printed in the USA
BVOW02s0305240916

463169BV00003B/55/P